BlindSight

To Pat: Grace is you
Soldier through

Jane L. Toleno

BlindSight

come and see

By Jane L. Toleno

Singing River Publications

Ely, MN 2006

BlindSight: come and see

ISBN: 0-9774831-4-2

Published by

Singing River Publications, Inc.
PO Box 72
Ely, MN 55731-0072
www.singingriverpublications.com

Author: Jane L. Toleno
Editor & Research Assistant:
Patricia Daily
Additional Editing: Islan Hejy
Cover Design & Layout:
Michael Wood; C Rolando Design
Photo, Back Cover: Dar Daily

Printed in Canada.

Alternative Formats:

For braille or tape formats contact The Communication Center, Minnesota State Services For The Blind, at (US) (651) 642-0500. For information on a commercial audio book version please contact Singing River Publications, Inc. at (US) (218) 365-3498.

DEDICATION

I dedicate this first book to my mom and dad, beloved caregiver Eula Lee, my brothers Bill and John, my older sister Anne, and my twin sister Mary Lee. We listened and talked together then. All our communications styles are here today.

ABOUT THE AUTHOR

Jane Toleno's passions are speaking and writing. She currently serves on a citizen's library accessibility review panel for the Minnesota Department of Education, and has served on other advisory groups in the past, including for the U.S. Library of Congress. Her activities include reading, church, community volunteering, spending time with family, and collecting books for troops overseas. Together with her husband Tom, she enjoys training Labrador retrievers to compete in AKC field trials and NAHRA hunt tests. She is thrilled when she gets an opportunity to participate in gatherings of writers, singers, square dancers, basket weavers, bell creators and bell collectors.

You may reach her through Singing River Publications.

CONTENTS

ACKNOWLEDGEMENTS

To Mom: We stand, arms linked together. Thanks for so many life-shaping, book-growing conversations. This book honors you.

To Eula Lee Neal: You were the unexpected, extra special other Mom in my life.

To Dad: Where yearning for what could have been and never was; where sorrow over missing you as a friend in my life exists, this book recognizes you.

To Bill: Hey Bro, I love you guy. Whether you could handle it or not, you were—and are—my girlhood hero.

To middle brother John: I hear you say, "Clear. Direct. Short. Lose those adjectives." Even though it is like pulling teeth for me, I get it. You saved the world from my infatuation with descriptors. Love you, John. Thanks for all the tandem bike rides we've shared.

To Anne: you older sister who terrorized and thrilled me. You were my first remembered example of the power of imagination at work, of "seeing" in different ways. Loved you while you lived and miss you now.

To Mary Lee: sister, twin, kinswoman, friend. Connected by circumstance and by the pure joy of choice. This book is for you, Sis. Thanks.

To Tom: Where learning to keep on through rough or smooth waters, where traveling together gives joy, there you are, friend and husband, help and love. Essential to me; the warmth and energy of a candle in my heart.

To our children Joanna and Dan, their life partners Ken and Tracie respectively and the four grandest creations ever: Kaylie,

Felicia, Vincent and Zandra. Sharing facts about our experiences together gives me more than joy.

To Dan DelGuercio, proprietor of Abbey Road Book Search: The timing of your questions was perfect. I couldn't resist them.

To Pat Daily: a beloved friend and writing, reading and technical assistant for this book who continues asking until I take risks to get clear about what I really mean.

To Molly and Vicky, Lolly, JP and Becca—kindred spirits truly!

To my Minnesota girl friends: Anne, Dee, Jan, Jean, Jodi, Julie, Pam, Pat, Wendy.

To the best neighborhood: we have shared the gift of helping raise the children around the cul-de-sac.

To editors and manuscript reviewers who taught me the value of periods sooner rather than later.

To Christine Moroni, President of Singing Rivers Publications. Thanks for your undaunting belief in me and this project.

To staff at Minnesota State Services for the Blind, especially Dick Strong, Stewart Holland, Mary Archer, Ellie Sevdy, Sally Winterle, Hal Schardin, and Charlotte Czarnecki.

To University of Minnesota instructors, program and support staff, especially Michael Dennis Brown, Becky Omdahl, Angelita Reyes, George Shapiro, Toni McNaron, Jacquelyn Zita, Beverly Atkins, Kit Gordon, Karen Murray Cruise, Amanda Roll Kuhne, Judith Wanhala, Brian Ruona, Jamie Tiedemann, Margaret Ottinger, Tim Kamenar, Tammy Swenson Lepper and Gene Chelberg.

To the Seeing Eye Incorporated: Throughout most of my adult life, your work with dog guides has empowered me. Thank you. And, true to form, this project is no exception. It is full of your influence.

To communities I love:

- To apple growers, basket weavers, bell collectors and square dancers everywhere.
- To bookstores, libraries, writers, readers and writing groups I appreciate and respect.
- To bus drivers and riders on Twin Cities buses.
- To dog guide users, American Kennel Club and North American Hunt Retriever handlers and dogs any time, anywhere
- To New Hope Animal Hospital and the University of Minnesota's Veterinary Teaching Hospital.
- To docs at Northwest Family Physicians and elsewhere, Northwest Eye Clinic and Davis Chiropractic Clinics.
- To Restorative Justice and Peacekeeping Circles everywhere.
- To early childhood educators and projects.
- Most of all, to my community of faith: Valley Community Presbyterian Church, whose mission statement declares, "Open hearts. Open minds. Opening lives to God." Thanks be for Dinners for Seven groups, Care Circles, Families Moving Forward and all the other opportunities for serving here.
- To Presbyterian Clearwater Forest and the vision that brought Clearwater Chrysalis into being for women of all ages.

CHAPTER ONE

Beginnings of My Journey: Finding the Right Words

During a recent phone conversation with a long-time friend and used-book seller—whom I have yet to meet face-to-face—a genuinely probing question about my physical blindness arose.

"With your permission, Jane, may I ask a really personal question?" asks my friend. "I really want to understand. What are dark, light and blindness like for you?"

Though this friend knows I am blind, until today's conversation, we'd simply enjoyed easy hopscotching from current affairs interests and personal concerns to talk of authors and books. We spoke of blindness only when details of book purchasing were involved—"Jane, what prompts you to buy print books?" or "Will you send a check… oh, how does check signing work for you?"

While asking his question that day, his tone of voice and words expressed deep caring and keen interest—qualities I genuinely appreciate and gladly respond to most of the time. The pauses between his words reveal his awareness of the new, personal—possibly private?—territory into which he sought access. He has never just talked and waited to talk some more.

This is a person who wants to share meaningful, and as it turned out, life-changing conversations.

But first, my friend waits; the silence between us deepens. Can he have any inkling of the layered situation developing at my end? The phone cord weaves through my fingers while his voice fades into the internal tumult of all the other voices that had sought to understand my personal and cultural experiences with dark, light and blindness.

Dismayed, I pull in a deep breath, cringe and wonder. Must I have this conversation again? I sure don't feel up for it. Don't I ever get to take time out from blindness? No. It's always here. It's always part of me. Why can't blindness be just a neutral physical thing? Why are its fingerprints found throughout my whole person, life and culture?

Briefly, intently, I want to be rid of this accidental yet permanent, personal and cultural marker. What would the whole person I am be without blindness as part of it? Would I look and act good—no, better than good—perfect—if I were not blind? Ridiculous! Blindness does not have to overwhelm me just because another person asks about it. I do not have to fear looking bad or being bad just because physical blindness resides in me.

What, I mentally fret, if this accidental difference transposes into a barrier to our friendship and categorizes me as irreconcilably different with a capital D?

Fears and memories converge, break away, then thrash about within me. Like trout, they rise from quiet depths to just under the surface of my pool. For the first time in years, I remember how immobile I often used to feel when children blatantly, but honestly, pointed out my blindness to their parents: "Mommy, why do her eyes wiggle? Why does she have that STICK (white cane) in her hand?" only to have those well-meaning adults hush them and hurry away. I consider again how people like me who live blind in a culture that sees can't help but disturb others' comfort zones. Our culture's sighted majority wants us to be normal—like they are—thus, I/we ought to be able to see, or at least act as seers do. But physical seeing simply will not ever happen for me. How can my culture even come to understand that I have a personal sense of wholeness when theirs so unrelentingly depends upon having all their faculties and senses present whether or not they intentionally make use of them? Can my culture risk understanding that my personal sense of wholeness depends upon having less than all my senses, appreciating and making intentional use of what I have all of the time? This "All I Have" includes each of my ways of knowing, the ways they work together and the information they provide me, a collective I have named BlindSight.

The longer I wait to speak to my friend, the closer to overload I get. The more the pressures build, the faster my silence shatters into what I call internal whitewater noise. When this inner turbulence tackles me, all boundaries between sensory input and perceptual knowing distort or dissolve. External and internal noises become one. I lose my balance. I slow down, stop moving altogether if I must. I wait to regain balance before moving ahead.

My reactions to this friend's questions? Way out of proportion. I struggle to integrate what is currently happening with making time to answer well. What to do? Blow him off with a light answer? Suggest a book? Write a book? Pick through the scattered thoughts and feelings rattling within me like seeds in a hollow gourd? I realized just how deeply I want my silences, words and actions to make a difference to the friend at the other end of the line. Truly I want him and others to be informed, understanding allies about disability activism. I want all Americans to recognize how disabilities are personal, yet shared; private, yet oh, so public. In these United States, disabilities are political, social, and economic experiences that we all must share, whether we want to, or not.

I sigh. Shake my head to send fears, memories and misgivings packing. Slowly move toward the conversation I knew could come if I let it. Oh, please, let this conversation bring connection into being. My shoulders shrug in capitulation. My jaw loosens, my tongue moistens. I open my mouth and begin.

"Oh boy," I finally muse aloud. "Light? Dark? Blindness? Easy questions? Hah! There are layers upon layers to sift and sort, name and blend here. But I think we have to talk about blindness before we can talk about light and dark."

My friend sounded pensive, stuck. "Layers of dark, light and blindness? What are they, and why so complex?"

Dear reader, if you, too, are curious, I welcome you to the dialogue in this book. Dip into these essays a little at a time, individually or sequentially. May these essays, like good conversations, enrich, enhance and open new space for you on your life journeys as they have mine.

CHAPTER TWO

Journey with Blindness: Blindness as Problem, Change Agent, Teacher, and now, Friend

Three months early, feet first, my twin sister and I breached Mother's threshold of pain and entered the world in August, 1947. We weighed just three pounds each. We were frail and unable to breathe on our own. The accepted medical practice at that time was to place premature babies in incubators until they were able to breathe independently. There we breathed a constant flow of pure oxygen. Though doctors believed that incubation and oxygen helped premature babies survive, unfortunately, during the late nineteen forties and early fifties, they did not know that too much oxygen could cause scarring of eye tissues, permanently destroyed retinas, and varying degrees of blindness. Over-oxygenating was further known to cause deafness and brain damage. Midway through the fifties, medical practitioners recognized that there were irrefutable connections between the amounts, constancy and duration of oxygen administered to premature infants and resulting degrees of blindness, deafness or brain damage.

What happens to preemies today? If oxygen is needed, it is monitored constantly with far less impact upon an infant's vision.

After several months of meticulous in-hospital and at-home care, Mom's uncertain concerns resolved into relentless, undeniable fears and suspicions.

"Something terrible is wrong with my girls' eyes."

In the ice and snow of winter, January, 1948, the pediatrician sent her to an ophthalmologist. During our first examination, we were wrapped in sheets to keep us still and prevent our hands from flailing.

After examining us, Dr. Kenneth Swan confirmed, "They are blind." With great empathy he said, "We just don't know yet how this happens. Other preemies appear to be blind as well."

Medically speaking, our blindness was permanent. No cures existed. The scars inside our eyes blocked the pathways for seeing. Those delicate, corrupted tissues could not be replaced. Nothing but maintaining the physical health of our eyes could be done.

Mom took us home; our family cared for us and loved us. Dr. Swan warned our parents not to take us back East for treatment. Doctors there would think that this was cancer; they might enucleate (remove) our eyes.

The collective medical knowledge and practice at the time couldn't cure or repair our eyes—nor could they replace them. Neither could it hand us off to rehabilitation and special education programs; they didn't exist yet. Dropped balls—eyeballs perhaps? Later, Dr. Swan gave Mom significant support. He told her to let us handle everything—let the girls put things in their mouths to develop their own awareness of relationships of texture to shapes. This was hard for her to do since we were young during a time when, if you wanted to be a good mom, you disinfected all things by boiling them before children touched or tasted them. Following Dr. Swan's advice forced her outside conventional practice, and it freed us to learn. From then until Mary and I left to go to college, we saw Dr. Swan as often as needed. We forged necessary yet uneasy alliances and friendships with Dr. Swan and staff.

When Mom's Dad, a Texas general practice doc and my Opa, asked, "Hester—Honey—are you ready to do all you can to help these babies survive?"

Her answer rang in that medical world then, as it rings in my life today, "Yes!"

Merely by existing and surviving this hospital accident, we girls turned many people's lives inside out and upside down. Recently, Mom described her initial sadness to me.

"Janie, for the first two years of your lives, whenever I talked to anybody about you girls, I cried."

And what did she do with this sadness? She let it motivate her to get to work on our behalf. Mom found that there were no education programs for blind preschoolers. She and other parents succeeded in identifying their own and their children's needs. They sought to provide play opportunities, created summer institutes for parents of blind children to promote social and daily living skills, and tirelessly worked to promote the passage of legislation that would affect policies toward education for blind children in public schools. It was never easy work. At one such meeting, an outraged woman approached Mom and ranted, "Why aren't you home taking care of those poor children?"

Her response? "Somebody has to do this and raise the money" and she went back to work.

How would blindness affect our family? Bother? Challenge? Tragic problem? Opportunity to live well and learn much? All of the above? Individually and together, we would have to discover this for ourselves. First, foremost and always, common sense, hope and courage prevailed. We were loved and cared for, helped and taught. Many parents of blind children coddle or curse them; they let physical difference distort and/or overrule the general good health and the promise of who their children might become.

Initially, though bewildered, our family and friends struggled to either ignore or make sense of our blindness. They stayed away—or were empathetic and got involved in our lives. They prayed for our healing—or accepted us as we were. They were angry and uncomfortable—or let their world be bigger because of us in it. They tried, not always appropriately, to help—or provided useful information. They suggested institutionalization—or helped fill our home with positive experiences. They spoke as if we were not in the room—or talked with and read to us. What a mixed bag of reactions.

We girls worked to make sense of and interact with people, places and things in our lives and our world like most infants everywhere—but I have since learned this was not true for many blind children. We naturally reached for human contact, listened to understand and learn, prattled at people for practice, walked places with people we knew. We handled things, sniffed, tasted, worked them with our hands, and put them in our mouths if we could. Without hesitation, we cataloged the textures, temperatures, weights, shapes, sizes and actions of everything we touched.

Early on, my little bit of working vision let me see big motions and large objects. I saw dark and light as in night and day, black, white and other bright colors. I dreamt, not in Technicolor but in impressions. My twin, with her greater amount of working vision, dreamt in visual pictures and color. Regrettably, in daylight or dreams, I never could see that tricky, "little shadow" that one of my favorite Robert Lewis Stevenson poems promised could "go in and out with me." No worries. My twin, who could see them, filled me in on the look of those long, slinky shadows or the stubby, short ones. Even without seeing, I most definitely had fun imagining this secret friend.

My glasses protected my eyes from physical harm. With slight magnification in one lens, they made my eyes look more uniform. They enhanced the vision I then had. Do I still wear glasses though I no longer have any vision? Yes. They add a sexy look. Also, my glasses give me some social distance from and protection against people's probing curiosity.

My twin sister's status as a legally blind/partially-sighted person means that her story unfolded differently than mine. She always tried gathering information with her eyes first, because she could see just enough to know that other people were seeing, and that seeing was the premier sense, even when hers was slow and unreliable. She chose to find meaning in what she partially saw and what she suspected. She was reluctant to use her other senses to collect input. She usually chose to hide her needs beneath pretences of looking with her eyes.

Kids being kids, one brother taunted, "Go ahead, Mary. Pick it up. You can see it, can't you??" No, she couldn't see it very well, but she wouldn't admit to that.

In elementary school, Mary and her teachers were caught up and divided by the two way struggle between reading print (large print, in ugly, heavy black and white books), or, learning braille (bigger, uglier, all white, full of dots, books). During our first grade and only year at the Oregon State School for the Blind, Mary and the one other partially sighted child were segregated. Teachers started her reading large print rather than braille. Because she could see a little, they thought this a good idea. The next year, when we entered the second grade at the public school near our home, teachers said to her, "Because of your poor vision and your slowness at print reading, you have to learn braille".

In third grade she was switched back to print again. And so the switching and her consequent isolation went. It didn't occur to anybody at the time that she could benefit from gaining both sets of skills.

When we were young, seeing, and how Mary had to work at it, bothered me. Why didn't she look with her hands, which I believed would have been faster and more accurate? Like me, presumably, she might have been more confident about what she saw and more competent in how she gathered information. I couldn't understand why seeing was so important, and why it counted for so much when she couldn't do it well, and I could hardly do it at all. It didn't even occur to me that others could see effortlessly until we reached school age. At that point, resentment took root in Mary. She didn't like the way my almost total blindness made my life simpler and it infuriated her that I could gain what she believed were privileges as a "blind" person. She intentionally chose to pass as sighted—but at what cost to her? Tremendously high costs, we now both agree.

Over the years, Mary Lee grew into her worlds—legally blind/partially sighted. Though she still resisted, she made a conscious decision to become proficient at using both her sight and sense of touch.

Today, my twin uses all of her working vision and shifts between print and braille. She uses a magnifying glass for reading small print, a monocular for reading distant print, e.g., street signs and building logos, and a note-taking computer to braille business and personal information. She integrates the use of print, braille, and audio formats with some ease, but never fluidly or casually—it's always difficult. In our adult lives we have talked of our different experiences with living blind until healing and reconciliation could come. Now, we trust each other's perceptions and styles. We have realized that some of our issues were far more about growing up than they were about being blind!

Meanwhile, as with children everywhere, each at our own pace, but together, we busied ourselves learning to get out and around in our world. Since nobody at home told me blindness might be a deterrent, I, the younger one of the moving and shaking Turner twins, moved. Blindness shaped some of the ways we did things. It did not stop us. We learned that slow approaches could provide useful time for investigation and action planning. We learned to tiptoe, jump, hop, skip (with or without skipping ropes), somersault, swim and dive, roller skate, tumble, and trampoline (can you tell I love motion?). When I crashed into things, I crashed. I usually remembered where they were next time. When our brothers teased by moving objects into our paths, we figured out ways to get back at them. If I could not get at them with a pinch, I tattled until they got in trouble.

Like other young children, we learned to dress and toilet ourselves. Tie our shoes? Where was Velcro when we needed it? We participated in the work of home: made our beds, put toys away, carried child-sized batches of laundry to drawers, and cooked with Mom and Eula. We learned to communicate in our world; bringing in the mail, answering telephones and doors were my favorite social jobs. We learned to sing and dance, speak, read and write, hold still, be quiet, wait when Mom told us to.

Mom intentionally made use of our natural actions in teaching us. She'd ask questions or make statements such as these: "Janie, where is that sound coming from? What does it tell you is happening? Where have you found that shape before? What smell is that? Think now, how high did you stack those cans last time before they fell?" and so on. She'd say, "Honey, use your words. Tell me something about that."

As long as I can remember, Mom's attitude was: My girls should grow up doing all they can and want to do when and wherever they want to do it. Blindness? Fit it into their lives day by day.

She tells me that these attitudes weren't always so. She grieved because she wanted for us the joys she'd experienced during high school: cheerleading, marching band and the like. "Janie, do you remember how we'd watch the Miss America Pageant each September? You kids would act out your talents; we'd pick our winners. When you were around eleven you wondered, if, when you were grown up, could you do that? I thought not, but didn't have the heart to discourage you, so I said, 'Maybe so'. I became a much better mother once I stopped wishing that you would have the same things in your lives that I had. You were having good lives of your own and I needed to support you in them."

One of the most important conversations I've had during my adult life with my Mom was when we happened to be talking about being mothers and children. It crossed my mind to tell her, "Mom, I do not hold you responsible for my blindness in any way." What a gift of reconciliation and forgiveness, acceptance and love we didn't even know we needed to share until that moment. What a revealing conversation followed: Mother with Daughter, Mother with Mother, Woman with Woman together.

Growing up, blindness was not ignored at home. Our eyes were freely spoken of in matter of fact words and tones of voice. Blind was a familiar descriptor of our eyes, as familiar as their chocolate brown color. Kudos and thanks, Mom, for your intuitive, then increasingly informed and practical stand on our behalf. I think it was right then; it was perfect—still is! All that big freedom of physical movement when I was young shaped my heart, my mind and spirit as I grew.

The day came when we girls devised a great new game which helped us to more fully understand that blindness and seeing truly differed from one another, and the people who could see had great advantages over us. The game went like this: after filling buckets with water at the kitchen sink, we would carry them to the front porch and then pour the water on the camellia and hydrangea bushes. On our second splashing trip through the house, Mother surprised us by saying, "Girls, stop."

Our third trip started out in conspiratorial whispers on slow stepping tiptoes. Mother's stern, imperative voice sounded: "GIRLS, STOP THAT!"

One of us stamped a foot and yapped. "How did you know what we were doing? Could you hear us?" Mother sat down on the floor and talked with us then.

"Janie, Mary, touch your eyes. Touch mine. All our eyes look alike—feel alike too. But our eyes are different. Your eyes do not see. My eyes do. This means that whether I'm nearby or far away, I can tell what you're doing, even if you're being quiet."

So that's the way it works, I thought. "Not fair," I said.

"No, it isn't but that is the way it is," Mom said.

Mom included us in buying groceries, mailing packages, choosing flowers to honor important occasions, and her work at Lewis and Clark College. We loved days spent at the Portland zoo, in the Macleay Park woods or the open spaces at Council Crest Park. Have you ever taken young, blind, twin daughters to a furniture auction? Our mom has. It was our first experience with armchair shopping. Impetuous, determined me, I loved it! Just poke your card in the air every time they offered a new item or price. Grab, grab, grab went Mom's hands to stop us from bidding, while her words described the action as fast as the auctioneer could rattle out his pitch. Mom wondered, do I really want to have my girls out in public? Is it OK? As always, she answered yes.

There was the memorable Easter Sunday morning when we arrived late to church. My brothers were dressed in itchy suits. Mary wore blue and I pink organdie dresses and crisp petticoats.

We wore flowery hats that sat on our heads like—please please don't fall off—mixing bowls or flower pots. We wore white cotton gloves that buttoned at our wrists; they may have been elegant but they blocked my finger eyes from ready seeing. We buckled patent leather Mary Jane dress shoes into place across the tops of our feet. Even now, the sounds of tapping leather heels gussy up the wearer in my mind. We carried white wicker basket purses with starchy petaled decorative flowers on top.

Arriving as late as we did, we made quite a scene. The only available seats were high in the hot, stuffy balcony. Right away, we girls began exploring our new environment—this wasn't our normal pew. These rows of seats were tiered. Mary was the first to spy an interesting, shiny, pink ball at close to perfect hand height. She stuck out a finger to explore it.

"What's that Mom? It's shiny. It looks like an Easter egg."

Mom made the first grab of the episodic morning.

I reached to see and help explain. "Mary, it's warm and smooth."

Grab number two. "Girls, I'll explain later."

"Jane," Mary whispered proudly, "I think it's a bald head? Now it's red!"

The man made such a fast escape that Mom never did get to explain to the gentleman, "Oh, it was just my girls learning." She was reminded again that when children needed to know, they think they need to know now. Waiting until later isn't always an option.

Outside our home, public preschool and kindergarten peers introduced us to ourselves as deviants and problems. Their actions made clear that the seeing culture was the only one that mattered. It's the standard against which all others are measured.

As long as you're blind, you'll be an outsider! Oh, how I got it. As long as I was blind, I was wrong in their world. Their fingers and everything about them pointed at us, pushed us away. Eyes that were accepted at home were wrong eyes most everywhere else. At their young hands, my eyes became my fault and problem. These different eyes of mine gave peers opportunities to tease, name call, and hide my glasses.

They said, "Jane, do you want to see this?" And when I eagerly turned my head to listen and reached to touch it, they'd wave it in my face and snicker. They said, "How many fingers do I have up?" while spreading their fingers against my face and pressing their palms against my nose.

Peers poked and pinched. They offered friendship and physical guidance (on double dares from others), then pushed me into half opened doors or coat hooks and ran out of reach.

They said, "You're amazing. Can you really tell colors by their smells? So does brown, like your eyes, smell poopie?"

They said, "You are really ugly!"

I cried; how I cried. My tears spewed out like the pressured water from a fire hydrant. They still sting to remember. Why do they say that? My eyes are blind. They are not ugly; they're brown! My eyes aren't all there is to me; there's lots more. My eyes are not like bad apples in the barrel of me. They're just blind is all! My body isn't blind or ugly!

For those kids, my eyes were just the beginning. They taunted, "Bad eyes! Bad body! Bad girl!" Much as I fought against such perceptions, I soaked them in. When young, I used to fight back by thinking, but for this accident of blindness in my life, I'd be perfect.

Without understanding it then, I believed that many children and some teachers were confused by my lack of visible scars combined with normal kid behaviors. They reasoned, if blindness is so terrible, why doesn't she look and behave in extreme and spectacular ways? They didn't know what to do with me. Teachers tried to offset kids' fear-driven treatment with syrupy benevolence. Truly special Jane (though she hadn't earned it—didn't want it—and attempted to act cute in response) was invited to be extraordinary, be first in line, sit here, give your book report first. Those special treatment messages carried more than words; they smacked of unearned privilege. Teacher voices spilled sweetness. Their pressing hands or pinching fingers conveyed their real mean-spirited messages: Do what we tell you—it's for your own good. All this damaged and cheapened the special treatment. Even though I performed the ordinary things the other kids did, I felt out of place, like dog-doo in the house. Were they stepping in dog-doo for the first time? I wished to be accepted and included for who I was–my own normal.

Episode by episode, teachers' words and voices invited, while actions tried to control. Those situations didn't contribute to my learning the kinds of social or intellectual skills I really wanted and needed in school. On any given day, I didn't know which would turn up first, nasty kids or nasty-nice teachers. How unexpectedly satisfied I felt the day I accidentally threw up on the mean kindergarten teacher's fresh-made row of easel paints. All that perfectly tainted blue, red, yellow, purple, green and orange.

Only six of my preschool through grade twelve years were positive and productive. During the 1950's and 60's, public education programs for disabled students were just coming into being. Looking back, I know that I was one of the truly fortunate ones. My fourth, fifth, and seventh grade teachers at Riverdale Elementary School insisted that I do every bit of the required and extra curricular work.

"So what if it takes you longer? So what if all your books are not taped, your work sheets not brailled and we have to read assignments out loud for you? So what if you have to have tests read out loud and we write your answers, or you have to type-write your tests while others use pen/pencils? We will find ways! So what if other students ask questions about your eyes? Ask them questions about themselves. Tell them you'd rather talk about something else today."

Because Mom and these teachers believed in me, I began to believe in me. The payoffs were stunning. My science project won a first place in Oregon's statewide science fair. I can still taste the metal, can feel the weights and sizes of the variously shaped magnets. With minimal assistance and supervision, I did my own work, placing horseshoe and bar magnets in different pairs and groups so that their positive and negative poles sat near or far from each other. I covered them with onionskin paper, sprinkled iron filings across each page, preserved them by spraying on varnish, then tactilely explored the varied patterns. I wrote about each attracting or repelling pattern and learned that I could do my own work. Along with other seventh graders, I ran our school's store, took the Red Cross first aid program, and participated in school plays and choirs. I won a first place in our speech contest and learned that I could prepare successful speeches with research achieved by interviewing subjects face-to-face or via telephone.

In addition to required academics, my sophomore, junior, and senior years in high school were a great blend of learning and extra-curricular activities. During these years, I belonged to school choirs and an ensemble, a folk singing group and a pep-rally club. I volunteered each Saturday as a counselor at a Portland area community center, the Neighborhood House. Time spent on the Lewis and Clark College campus, where Mom taught and later was the Dean of Students, contributed to my curiosity about the wider world. My determination to explore and experience it first-hand as my circles of friends widened countered the sharp pain of destructive comments.

At an eighth grade school dinner dance, boys replaced my food-filled dishes with their dirty ones and didn't ask me to dance unless told to by chaperones. Or, during one of my annual spring vacation visits to my Newman, California, high-school-teacher-Dad, a certain young Prince Charming responded to his mom's invitation for me to stay for supper by saying, "No, she can't," just as I enthused that I'd love to. On our silent drive back to my Dad's apartment, Prince Charming explained that he was afraid I'd embarrass him—spill, or something.

Further on in high school I encountered a challenge of another sort. An instructor commented, "You don't need to take science and higher math subjects. You won't need them."

Occasionally, during my teens and early twenties, defiance and personal rage caused me to deliberately test or abuse the very systems intended to help me move forward. How often—far too often—well-intended actions and people have harmed rather than helped in my life. There was my first experience with authority outside my family after I left home to attend Syracuse University. When I was told to submit all textbook fees, course selections, and textbook costs to the state rehabilitation department, I got mad. I'll show you. Who the heck are you anyway? Who makes up your rules? Why do your rules apply to me? Why do I have to report my purchases and course selections to you? I don't even know you; you are not my boss! I retaliated by choosing an interesting elective they hadn't recommended, an art history ideas course. In one brilliant spending spree, I brazenly bought many hundreds of dollars worth of intriguing, but completely unnecessary visual collections of paintings and "gave them" to peer readers to peruse. My mom had to pay for the books, which never did come back. One lesson for me lay in the reality that other people had very definite ideas and the money and power to back them up about what I could do. The bigger lesson was that my "I'll show you" choice hurt my mom and me, and I had to learn that there are times you must work with those you don't like.

During these same years, I was determined to discover for myself how sexual things worked. When was it permissible for me to get personal, to learn about my body as a sexual entity on my own terms? When would I—how could I—gain any sense of what I looked like? When might discovering the ways the rest of the world operates make room for self discovery? I really felt that I could find self-awareness through touch. What if I get caught? Oh, why does this culture in which I live demean honest touch so? Hands, I entreated, inform the rest of me. Mind, give me correct and respectful ideas and language to name what my hands learn. Spirit and feelings, teach me to have confidence and take wise delight in what my hands show me. Body, you mover, give me new acts to put into words; give me more language of being and doing.

During my late teen years, I lived in Syracuse, New York. I opted to model for community college art classes to earn money and connect with live art communities. In addition to resolving these practicalities, far more fortunate learning resulted. I had to stay awake and hold my poses. Curiosity, please go to work. Turn up something interesting for me to think about while from my head to my toes my body held each aching position.

I heard thrilling snippets of art instructor and student talk. "The way she's facing gives me a clear connection with her energy. Makes her available; keeps us distant. No facades. It's like nothing's hidden—we get a lot of power, energy, mood. See the musculature of her arm and shoulder—see the shadow there? Work them together. How do we draw that interest of hers; the curious tilt of her head? Look at how Jane's posed. Is she going to jump? Get that intent. Hmmm. She has a natural, strong look. When she touches her face—around her eyes—she looks sorrowful. Looks simple to draw because she's so there—it's really difficult—complicated."

What comfort these affirming comments were for my yearning to have a sense of how I looked. Perfect? No. Imperfect? No! Right for me? Yes! Now I could claim authentic sense of my own appearance. And is there any woman on earth who doesn't want to know the powers and joys of her own beauty, first-hand? Personal beauty or image does not have to be a protective, coat-like layer that people take off or put on for public consumption. Image—my image—really can come from inside–generated from who I am, what I do, feel, think, wish or want. I do not have to convince others that I'm alive by facing their direction with alert or interested facial expressions every minute. Bodies or faces whose quiet or stillness is focused do not communicate blank empty minds, hearts or spirits. My life experience reveals that quiet and stillness can clearly communicate respect. They can offer space in which others can finish what it is they happen to be considering; give everyone time to hear and sort through it; provide gear-shifting and choosing opportunities. Then and there I decided if others wanted that exterior look, let them have it! Not for me our culture's persistent promotion of defining our lives based on what is seen. Not for me, the glossy-as-magazine-pages glaze.

Here are some of the ways I see myself: clean, clothed, comfortable with my body, with a clear mind and open spirit, available, engaged, sturdy, and glad. Imagining myself with the qualities and looks of a sturdy Bonsai cedar, a bronze or silver bell, the power of one feather to balance and propel a bird all give me delight and courage. Picturing my being as a green, red or yellow apple with a star pattern of creative, productive seeds within gives me hope. These realities make a pretty incredible basis for self-concept, don't you think?

No divides as I mature or change. No incomprehensible social distances to navigate because of misinterpreting designer appearances. No more looking good by visual standards only. No more will I ignore the information my hands and other senses can gather at the expense of maintaining approved visual and social distance. Blind eyes do not mean that "nobody's home" inside. They simply are eyes that do not see.

In contrast, my hands are my "see-ers". Out-there, moving hands are not inappropriate or out of place. My hands and I belong. They are full of purpose and style; they're in front of me—reading, writing, doing the work of my life, and bringing the future into my present! I get some of my favorite well-being, public relations images from my hands. I delight in how my hands serve me as ambassadors of good touch and thorough observation. It pleases me to know that they move well in the world; they depict me as graceful. A friend said recently, "Your hands approach things like a pianist." These information gatherers of mine are discrete yet fearless, willing to wait yet bold. My hands bring dreams from out in front of me where the future is into my here and now. My hands, with all they hold and represent, parade through my mind, my spirit and life; they declare themselves as out there creative and productive in the world.

A camera in my head creates a gallery:

Click. Fan hands touch topics—ignite conversation sparks—kindle bright, hot dialogue flames. No educated smoke screens or hissing hush-hush noises to dampen the fires of learning. Up goes my hand with yet another question.

Click. Broom hands with purposeful, powerful strokes sweep away confusions. No more "Which way does that E chart face?" Who cares? I do not. No longer does that knowing affect my worth.

Click. Dancing hands in fluent motion, speaking and singing with respectful authority and joy. No longer hands that grope, fumble or stumble as they gather information, read braille, perform tasks or see for me.

Click. I imagine filigree webbing between those fingers of mine. Dream catchers now. Hands, mistresses of Tai Chi, float down like ash leaves in autumn; they come to rest in the blessing bowl of my lap.

My first efforts to match personal choice in dress with the gallery of images in my mind shocked my mom. I went to college with wool skirts and sweaters, slacks and jackets, girdles and curlers. I sold it all. I returned for my first holiday with flowing, long and loose hair. My blue denim shirt (to this day I love denim) loosely lay over my braless torso. Marvelous hand-made leather sandals precisely fit to my feet; long braided ties wound up my jean-clad legs. Everything I needed was stored in a pack basket whose craftswoman I knew. In addition to sitting cross-legged on the floor, I hunkered down, hippie-style, sitting on my haunches. Mom reacted.

"Jane Livingstone Turner, where are your clothes?" she said, pushing away what she called a hamper that I carried on my back. "Where are you? Who are you?" She paced and her silence roared. Thanks, Mom, for the huge, unadulterated response.

The point? I could—and did—buy clothing without my mom's help that would express my self image, people would react, and we'd all survive. Over time, I revisited childhood memories of dressing up prettily as I had that Easter morning; I experimented with accessories and/or cosmetics that could enhance, nurture and protect rather than cover up my natural features. Image: collaboration of inside and out. What fun to try on all the things others see and accept/reject them as I choose.

And what about the dating scene—social gatherings? My oldest brother always counseled, "Remember, everybody's got to pee. So just ask for directions or an escort to the bathroom." Easy for you to say, brother dear, I thought. I'm the one who has to work it out.

More big social questions arose just after Tom, my husband of thirty-seven years, and I met. Can I flirt from a distance? Well, shoot! Flirt at all? I most assuredly felt the energy, took the challenge. Without seeing, I had to ask myself whether or not I thought I could overcome social distance without eye contact. Could this attractive fellow and I successfully travel toward deeper friendship and physical intimacy? Would walking together, my hand tucked under Tom's elbow in correct sighted guide position, be misunderstood?

When longing made room for loving, and we chose intimacy, I simply said, "I can't be sure my face will tell you what the rest of me feels ... does it? ...Does the good news show?"

Over time, Tom and I discovered that, when at gatherings, an upbeat "Yoo-hoo, Tom" across a crowded room, followed with a smile and a wave, or a "Hey Jane" from him to me, sufficed to keep us connected. When seriously needing to hook up with him in a crowd when I couldn't find him, I quietly asked others, "If you see Tom will you let him know I'm looking for him?"

Tom and I met in March 1965 when we were twenty-one and seventeen respectively. We dated for two years, broke up, got back together the summer of 1969, and were married in November. During those years, one discussion item we never disagreed about was that we loved, wanted and would share the work and joys of children.

Four years later, we prepared for the exciting event of the birth of our first child. High time to get down to practicalities: find role models, face fears and ask questions. I thought a lot about Mom—how it was for me as a child and her as my Mom. Decided what I would do the same, different or possibly better, brash novice that I was. I was going to be a stay-at-home mom while Tom earned income for us. I prepared for my role by gathering parenting tips from anybody who'd nurtured me and other caregivers I encountered. I asked family, friends and professionals—well, shoot—I asked people on porches, at grocery store checkouts, at bus stops and on buses about everyday baby things such as diapers, bathing, nursing, feeding, skinned knees, sickness and tantrums. Once I asked a likely suspect with a friendly, lower pitched and slightly rougher voice a question, only to hear, "I'm a boy—I haven't nursed a baby, yet."

I discovered that all those mothers with whom I spoke made it through; differently to be sure, but they made it through. Speakers expressed reoccurring themes such as, "You're not the first mother who's ever walked the planet. You'll get the job done." I took heart from the common sense, humor and creativity, the courage, faith, good luck and steadfastness that shone clearly in all accounts. If, whatever the challenge, they could do it, so can I. A valued, encouraging and energizing lesson I've kept with me since.

Our first major baby purchase: five-dozen square, hospital quality, flannel diapers, several sets of diaper pins, a bucket and lid for the dirty ones. I made it a habit to pile the freshly washed diapers in a flat stack on top of the clothes dryer as soon as I took them out of the machine. Fold as needed was my motto. Before Joanna's birth, I practiced folding them until the process flowed as smoothly as a good dance. "Bet I can fit any diaper to whatever shape bottom our baby has."

How could I keep from puncturing my child? The friend I asked had advised, "Jane, slide the diaper pins through your hair. They'll pick up your natural body oils and be much easier to push through those double-thick, nighttime diapers." What about those diapers that were mess-to-beat-all-messes? It only took a few memorable hits and smears to convince me that some situations were best contained by handling them in the bathtub.

And what of feeding children? I decided to nurse my baby to age twenty-one if necessary. For the record, I stopped nursing each of our two children when they turned one. Nursing, for me, had its own rewards. I gained confidence. When we started spooning cereal into Joanna, I'd put her in my lap with her back to me, cover us both with a towel, place my arms over hers to prevent grabbing little hands, dip the spoon in the porridge and bring it toward her face. She quickly adapted to leaning forward to get it. Then, we moved onto her facing me and handling food for herself while seated in her high chair. I simply didn't allow playing with food. It was my mom, Gramma Hester to our kids, who handed Joanna her first cup of water. Joanna never drank from a bottle.

Keeping Joanna dressed simply, in one piece outfits, solved problems of care free, easy off/easy on clothing. Only challenge was the fastening. Quickly, I realized that perfect snapping or buttoning wasn't going to make me a perfect mom; it wouldn't harm anyone if mismatches occurred.

Along with crawling and walking came exploration and play. In whatever room I needed to be, we organized cabinets or drawers full of kid toys. Alas! Pots, pans, cookie cutters, rolling pins, utensils and Tupperware quickly took first place in her interests. If Joanna, followed twenty-one months later by Dan, played in other rooms, the commonly enforced rule was when Mommy calls, you answer. Was it hard for them to play hide and seek? No, all they had to do was stand still, be quiet and try not to laugh too hard.

Fortunately, the first yard they played in was fenced. Learning along with them, the kids and I grew confidently able to exist at distances from one another.

There came the summer morning a visitor exclaimed in a horrified, DO-SOMETHING tone, "Jane, they're putting dirty crab apples in their mouths."

My responsive rather than reactive comment impressed even me, since my fear of missing something pertinent to their care was so deep and strong. "You know what? If they're too sour, they'll spit them out."

When Joanna and Dan were young, I traveled with a white cane. Dog guides didn't enter our lives until the kids were almost twelve and ten respectively. I didn't use a stroller—couldn't keep my kidlets safe when they were that far ahead of me. First front carry, then back carry rigs were the ticket. Later we'd go, cane tapping along out front, one child in a baby-carry pack and the other toddling beside, hand in mine or in my pocket.

Once they both walked, several afternoons weekly a high school or college student and I took the kids to the park where the student watched out for them during hours of free play. We switched from me carrying them to using the big red wagon—another of these timely gifts from Gramma Hester. One day the wagon tipped and tumbled them down over the curb. They cried over their now-dirty apples rather than their spill.

During our two-mile wagon pull to and from swim lessons, we created a game that I called Block Eyes. At each corner, child one, the front rider, hopped out, came forward and placed her or his left hand in my right side pocket. Child two, the back rider, jumped down and helped lift the back end of the wagon down, then up the curbs. They switched spots at the beginning of each block. All the way along we listened and noticed what was happening to us and in our surroundings. I taught them poems or Bible texts. We made up new songs or sang familiar ones, played guessing games, munched apples or other snacks.

Once they started school, the baby carriers and wagon were put away. They switched to bikes and left me walking in their dust. They still stopped at the end of the block and waited for me—or biked back to accompany my walking.

I also introduced them to bus travel. Then we were able to go to library story hours, children's theaters and other downtown events. It was a really special treat when Tom invited us to hop in the truck and go with him to bid on a carpentry or tree surgery job. Weather permitting, we would take a picnic along so that we could stop at a park before or after and make a day of it.

When Joanna or Dan showed interest in new things, such as electric plugs, I paid attention. We held plugs, named their parts and identified what they could safely hold. They saw where plugs went and learned what they did. We noticed that the prongs just fit into the socket holes. I declared, "Nothing else must go there—no fingers, no pencils, no Bobbie pins—nothing but the plug prongs. Got it?" They must have listened, because neither ever got shocked.

How did I know when my kids were getting sick? Their words or actions made it plain. Tom's visual assessment concurred. Here's how administering oral medication, eye, ear or nose drops happened: Depending upon what medicine had to be given, the patient got to sit or lie down on whichever surface he or she chose: kitchen counter or table, bed, chair, couch, or rug. We celebrated their choices as helpful. Pouring medicines into spoons never worked for me. Either I used a dropper or an old wide-mouthed crystal shot glass that had raised measurement lines inside and out. "Ready? Open. Take. Swallow. Atta way. You're the best." When drops were the item for dispensing, one orienting, stabilizing hand cradled the child's face while the other did the deed.

Illness wasn't always pretty, and it wasn't always fun. One time when Joanna had the stomach flu, she decided that she could make it to the bathroom in time—which she did. I met her there, held her head, rubbed her back, soothed her fears, and congratulated her on making it to the toilet, only to hear her wail, "But I didn't get the lid up!"

Another time Joanna bumped her head while chasing her brother through the house and told me there was blood. When we couldn't stop the bleeding and I couldn't reach Tom, I called a friend to take us to the emergency room. Poor Tom came home to blood smears, no one home to explain what had happened, and having to wait for a call. At the hospital, they took Joanna from me to suture her—but also to ask her leading questions such as, "Did you mother hit you?" Was this our culture's growing awareness of child abuse at work, or was it something more immediately ominous for me? The unspoken and pervasive perception being played out was that blind women can't properly care for their children. I never did completely get rid of the underlying fear that my children would be taken away from me if I didn't demonstrate good mothering by good physical care.

In addition to parenting, what about the world of work and my place in it? From my early years, work was something I knew about and did solo or together with others in my family. "See what I can do? I did it! You can count on me," were sentences I remember being glad I could say. Work often took priority over other activities; it could be hard, and I could begrudge it. "It's not fair. Make Danny (my brother John) do the dishes. Jumper (my oldest brother's nickname) can take the garbage outside." Though I'd rather have spent time talking or listening to people's stories any day, I had to learn to stick with jobs until they were finished.

There were some jobs they said I couldn't do, like mowing the grass. Sometimes work was fun—making applesauce, Christmas cookies or taffy, packing for picnics or trips with Mom. Sometimes I got paid for my work—Mary and I made and sold potholders, and we both babysat in the neighborhood—but mostly we did work because that's the way our family did things. Jobs needed to be done, and we needed to do them.

It never occurred to me as I matured that I wouldn't find occupation beyond the borders of my family. Work and play were expected parts of life. During high school, weekly volunteer work at a city community center and counseling at a summer day camp deeply satisfied me. My first real paid job was as a camp counselor at an Easter Seals Camp. During and after my Syracuse University years, I worked as an art class model, then as a teaching aid in a residential facility for multiply handicapped children. After Tom and I were married, I have been employed outside our home at various times. I was the first blind person hired by the New Jersey Bell Telephone Company, who did a remarkable job of adapting their equipment so that I could serve as an intercept operator. I have worked as a receptionist, a teaching assistant in early childhood education and child care settings, and a crisis hot line responder. In each of these positions, I was hired because I was job qualified and was not given special treatment. Any equipment modifications that were necessary were accomplished with minimal cost to the employer.

I learned early that work is the coming together of competencies to get jobs done. The more carefully and competently I accomplished routine work, the freer my mind and spirit could be to wander to other concerns. No wonder that, as an adult, I thoroughly enjoyed the technical college year-long, skills-based Child Development Assistant Program curriculum. I learned how to plan, set up, guide, support, assess, and clean up after activities were complete. I relished asking myself, "What parts of this learning activity would I do the same or differently? Why or why not?"

Now I have redefined for myself what it means to be fully employed. Whether as a volunteer or paid employee, commitment to perseverance and excellence makes the difference. Today I am a self disciplined and motivated speaker and writer; I value these opportunities as essential pieces of my work in life. Need a speaker or essay about blindness and employment? Blindness and parenting? Blindness and recreation or learning? Blindness and aging, culture, or race? Blindness and anything? Call me.

Living blind is a lifelong task for me, since my blindness is permanent. My working definition of permanent is that permanent cannot be undone, will be here as long as I will be. It is always visible, so it cannot be denied. Remember, I am blind everyday. I do not want to be described as differently abled, handi-capable, a survivor or the like. Blind will do.

On good days, I affectionately give my eyes a pat; say "All righty then, you hood ornaments, you No See 'Em girls. Get out from under foot and let me get my stuff done". With a grin, I sing to them that old song, "My beautiful, beautiful brown eyes" For me now, seeing is that precious sensory gift and process I participated in a bit when young but no longer find essential in my life. Been there, done that. Now and then, I mourn and miss it as a cherished something I used to have.

I miss colors that grab my full attention. I picture flavors of tangy apple green, juicy red, rich gold and ripest yellow. Vivid bluebell, blue bonnet, and cool bluebird blue live in my memory. Buttercup, daffodil, Johnny-Jump-Up, and pansy-center yellow cheer me and light my way. Red robin and red mitten red make me sing. Snowflake white and dewdrop clear speak to me of transforming grace. I affectionately promise my eyes, maybe somewhere down the road, in my next life, you'll see, and I keep on keeping on.

Here are a few telling lines from an early poem of mine.

BAREFOOT BEING

When roles and rules, when clothes and shoes
Flap on me—they do not fit!
I shuck them off today to be barefoot again.
I have five truths:
I am alive. I am barefoot.
I am blind. I am a worthy woman
And, God is here.
But my bare feet get snubbed and stubbed.
They get kicked and broken.
They have been lost. They get ignored
But they find my way.
The world says, "They are ugly!"
Now and then my tears or the tears of friends or the tears of God wash them
And they keep on walking.
Bare feet are the truths I have.
So, not to break these fragile truths,
(They are the first. Are they my last ties of human being?)
I test, I choose the roles, the rules,
The clothes, the shoes that fit
And my bare feet keep on keeping on.

Do I miss seeing moods and smiles? Now and then. Especially when, for whatever reasons, I fear missing out on them and forget to take time (and I do forget sometimes) to trust my own observational skills. Am I curious about facial expressions and body language? Sure, why wouldn't I be? See-ers are often shocked when we talk about what they see or what I "see". See-ers discover that they typically speak of appearances and surfaces and distances first; for many, only and always. They may/may not get further or closer, and they often don't care if they do. I notice information gathered with my senses: skin textures and odors, soap and perfume aromas; how people walk, stand, use or share emotional, physical or social spaces; how clothing and footwear fit to the person's movements; how people speak and treat others. I am interested in attributes or qualities inherent in the person, place, situation or thing.

A friend and I recently spoke about a person we'd just met. My friend summarized, "She's really fat. I wonder what's wrong with her."

I said, "Hmmm. Didn't sound bulky to me. And even if she was, she sounded glad when she laughed. Her comments showed real interest in the rest of the people in the group. She was quick to help others—you know, get information, suggest connections and the like."

Living blind, could I still find authentic ways to participate in the activities enjoyed by the people I love? How about it, BlindSight of mine, will you get me there? My philosophy is "I can't see it, so I have to get involved to get it". Our son, a captain of his high school wrestling team, addressed the audience during the end of the season banquet. Dan thanked me and said, "Mom, you've been at every wrestling meet from grade school on. You read amateur wrestling guides to learn the moves; tried them out on me and Dad at home to be sure you understood. You made friends with other families all over the Midwest. Our cheerleaders taught you some of their cheers. Nice move, Mom. Should have tried it myself. We couldn't score with them. Joke! You stood mat-side and followed each match; listened to team members giving play by plays. You cheered! So what if you were always ten seconds late. You always got it!"

On good days, living blind goes smoothly. It merely requires working out kinks when physical blindness meets life. Choosing personal organization underpins greater senses of personal freedom, choice and independence for me. I can take better care of myself, make connections when I wish or need, and find what I want when I want. Can I opt for laziness? Not often. Blindness hasn't let me. Paying attention to people and details of my surroundings requires that I be on high alert at all times. Thus, I maintain better personal safety. Mobility aids such as dog guides or white canes are necessary for independent travel as would be more sidewalks in place of so many shoulderless roads. Aids such as marking dots affixed to household appliances increase my efficiency. Print information in accessible formats and additional time when required all facilitate my getting a job done. Living blind in this twenty-first century means making effective use of technological aids such as cellular phones and screen reading computer software programs. And, at the end of each day of handling such challenges and choices am I weary? Oh, yes! Do I look forward to the next day? Usually!

Wherever I go, whatever I am doing, opportunities arise for answering people's questions about living blind. Most of them are what I call "good curious" but some are outrageous. Truly, many people think that it is perfectly acceptable to ask disabled people personal questions that would be impolite under most circumstances. I have had people whom I barely know ask me things about my sex life. Something about blindness seems to liberate people from many social constraints. Once, while visiting an area church, a woman walked directly up to my husband Tom, stared into his eyes and blurted, "Are you blind, too?" His response, with a laugh, was "No", but he wished that he had had a better comeback.

People ask me who picks out my clothes, dresses me, cooks and cleans for me. They ask with whom I live, if I dated, earn a living, how could I possibly be married, have reared children and have grandchildren. They ask my husband and children what it's like to have a blind person in their lives and if I do anything without their assistance. It helps to maintain a sense of humor in the face of these assumptions; I understand that people are curious. I can honestly answer peoples' questions, and sometimes we laugh together at misconceptions. Others have told me that my approachability gives them peace and makes them feel unafraid in a world where difference exists. These kinds of conversations have transformed my life from blindness as a burden to blindness as a blessing that I can share with others.

Consider our two children. In addition to the usual developmental challenges, Joanna and Dan faced the presence of their Mommy's disability in their lives. When Joanna was five and Dan almost four, we moved to a new neighborhood. My children cut lilacs from our bushes and trooped from house to house selling them "to get money to help our blind Mom." What thoughts, words and actions of others conjured up those concerns in their imaginations?

Shortly thereafter, we three were downtown doing errands. I tripped over my sandal-shod foot and fell. An indignant lady barreled up to us blurting, "Why aren't you children helping your Mom?"

The protective tigress in me exclaimed. "They didn't trip me. I tripped my big self! And where does it say in their job description that it's their job to keep me from harm every time?" And there you have a particular challenge. Like all families, we had to work through how and when to help one another. My fierce personal battle centered on being seen as a mom whose disability was not her children's responsibility while, at the same time, being a mom who enrolled her kids in being perceptive glad helpers.

In first grade Dan punched a child out who called his mom a dumb blind woman. Didn't I say that people who share the educating work might not always do what's polite? I have to admit, a small, intense part of me felt all shiny with pride at Dan's fighting to protect his mom's honor. Another part of me fought shame that he had to fight for the blind rather than glory or God and country.

Educating the public is always a challenge. I take all the help I can get in this endeavor from aware family members and trusted friends. Consider the dog guide situation: my dog and I have been accosted many times by well-meaning people who erroneously think it is all right to interact with a dog guide at work. For those of you who are not familiar with dog guide etiquette, be advised that you should never try to pet or distract a working dog of any kind.

From sixth grade on, when Joanna and I went places together, we flipped quarters to see who would do the dog guide and public conversations.

"My turn," my then-ninth-grader reminded as we jabbered our way through a nearby shopping mall. "Here comes a man, probably the dad, and two little kids."

As the man approached we heard him tell the children, "Here's how this works." He blocked our way. My dog briefly paused before responding to my "Hup!" command by side-stepping around him. "Hup" means pay attention, keep to your work.

The man said, "Your dog's sniffing me," and began petting him.

Joanna reached across me, brushed his hand away and retorted, "If you'd get your dick out of the dog's face and ask my mom first, she might let you meet him!"

Rude? Yes. Brash? Without doubt! Speechless, me? Why not? Nothing I could say could improve on, or repair that at the time! But later, Joanna and I would have to talk about that one. Part of me admits that I'd love to have said the very same thing to him. And yet? You do have to be civil. Educators come in all kinds of packages and use all kinds of language.

Without missing a beat, Joanna turned to the young children to invite, "Would you like to meet my mom's dog? Here's how you do it."

Now it's your turn to learn—here's how to meet a dog guide who is in harness and working. If possible, approach the person who is blind from the "off dog" side (the side opposite to where the dog is). Do not make eye contact with the dog. Introduce yourself verbally to the person. Ask for permission to pet the dog. Accept the answer given, even if it's no (most dog guide handlers will say no). If permission is given, keep it short—the dog is on the job.

As a person living blind, it is important for me to make the most of moments to connect anytime, anywhere. Imagine this: I stood in the communal shower after a workout at my club. My dog guide lay just beyond the door.

"Are you Jane Toleno?" came the tentative but determined question from under a nearby shower head.

"Yes, I am. And who may you be?"

She explained who she was and what she wanted.

Without hesitating, with my formal manners in place while that hot water luxuriously sluiced over bare skin, I extended a hand her way, "Well, how do you do. I'm glad to meet you." Then we burst out laughing at the picture we made.

Recently a woman made a tentative approach to me. Without saying anything first or identifying herself, she repeatedly patted and stroked my arm. I turned to her with a brusque command, "Don't do that."

She pulled her hand away as if she had been burned, which cued me that I needed to temper my reaction with humor. I smiled and said, "That makes me feel like I'm your lucky rabbit's foot. It also scared me." We laughed and got on with the business of sharing what works best: a word of greeting as you approach—"Hey, Jane, ..." or "hello..."—do a splendid job of acknowledging your presence. A brief touch to my shoulder quickly orients me to you, and vice versa.

Picture a swim and fitness club, dog guide on the floor in front of the bench of lockers where I sit dried but not yet dressed. A woman approached and knelt near my dog. Aware of this unannounced intrusion, I hopped off the bench, squatted down and intently faced her with a look. "You have a question?" She did.

And just for practice in protecting my freedom to not always be the educator-in-residence, I recommended, "Stop at the front desk and talk with Colleen; she'll answer your questions about how things work for me here at the club." Good thing Colleen and I'd covered that in previous conversations. I really can choose to answer questions directly or not at all; I can route them to other trusted allies if I wish. And, I can, I do, remember that conversations matter.

Imagine this: My dog curls down next to me and places his head on my foot. I sit on a bus bench at the end of an extra long and tiring university day. My mind is full. I appreciate the familiar backdrop of routine rush hour city sounds. They allow me uninterrupted sorting time. A person approaches. Leather heels tapping, the encroaching perfume and first words lead me to suspect she's female. There is plenty of empty bench space, and that increases my annoyance at how close—way too close—she sits. Her foot touches the back end of my dog, lying right at my feet. Our conversation goes like this: Stranger: "That's a beautiful animal. What's its name?"

I opt to play with the situation rather than yawn and show my disinterest. "Baxter. What's yours?"

"Nancy." (Does it matter that I have a name, too, or that I might not want to talk today?)

She pauses to think, then asks. "How old's Baxter?"

"Four. How old are you?" (Maybe that was rude—slap my hand.) I half turn my body, which shifts my dog's position and creates a little more wanted distance between us. She still isn't catching on. I can't wait to hear what's coming next.

"Is Baxter a boy or girl?"

"He's a boy—and you …?" (I know that was rude—now I'm really glad Mom's not here!) I then stand and walk to the curb to resume waiting.

Presently, in my late fifties, I don't even want to get rid of this accidental but permanent marker in my life—physical blindness that began with some working vision. Because of an incorrect diagnosis and handling of an unexpected eye trauma in the late nineteen eighties, my blindness is now total. Do my eyes hurt or bother me much? No. They cause little physical pain. Does my heart ache its way through all these experiences now and again? Yes! And ultimately, I continue my evolutionary journey from blind child on into and through legally, totally blind adulthood. Thanks to disability legislation, such as the Americans with

Disabilities Act (1991), I'm also legally present as a person with a disability! Proud of it, too!

And what of that "bad eyes, body and bad girl blind person" school mates too quickly, so thoroughly pointed out long ago? I'm happy to volunteer as a healthy, clean living, good-looking alternative body image for women any time, anywhere. Jane with juice! Strong as a feather. Helpless as a Mac truck. More grit per inch or ounce than sand paper ever had. Sturdy and flexible as a Bonsai tree, with such a root system and so many branches reaching high and wide! I cherish being sturdy. I am, will always be, an evolving fusion of normal and abnormal, of alike and different. Despite all the attention I've given to daily life and disability, do I have any clue what's ahead and how I'll handle it? No. Do any of us? I do know that age related disabilities will likely be part of my life. I do know this: To walk and talk with people is a better way for me to get the job of living done.

And what has ever happened to that white-water noise I told you earlier could overwhelm and unbalance me? I have come to recognize it for what it is—the flood noise of all the insider reasons I gave myself for coping with situations and surroundings by capitulating to, rather than collaborating with them. Now I take the time I need to assess what's happening. I celebrate that, without seeing, with BlindSight on the job, I trust my own disability-inclusive assessments and my sense of shared interdependence when I gather and use input from others. Voices from my past are done—in fact, I accept my entire past as a gift whose time of influence is complete. Old frightening sounds of internal white-water noise haunt me now and then. In those moments, I acknowledge them. Tell them they can hush now, put what I need out there. With dignity, I choose to picture each assertion as a fine Old Town canoe or pieces of faithful bread cast upon the water of human choice and experience.

CHAPTER THREE

Journey through Seasons: Where Light and Dark Meet

If blindness is the absence of light and dark from my life, then why can't I let them simply be absent? Why do I even think or care about them? Not seeing dark and light does not lessen their existence, importance or value to me. In fact, the opposite is so. They exist. They matter. They are valuable—even to, especially to—me as proof that I understand and function successfully around acceptable markers in my culture and the world. Here is how I know them.

My personal ways of knowing and experiencing natural dark/light, day/night and seasons are many. I know them by when and where they happen in the physical world. Every aspect of me knows them—body, mind and spirit, senses and emotions encounter them. Beyond my natural connections to light, dark, day, night and seasons, I know them via abstract, intuitive and symbolic, metaphorical and metaphysical experience. Their energies, moods and work declare who they are. Each one has sounds and silences, smells and tastes, temperatures and textures. I love the ways dark and light, day and night and seasons move; the ways time measures or marks, shifts or steps, or even holds still.

Sometimes softly, sometimes loudly, dark turns east toward morning. It warms and lightens through sunrise; it heats and brightens into the time of light we call day. This partnership of light and time winds west toward sundown, deepens, then dims and thickens, sometimes cools into dusk. It circles into dark, and then day is done. This chunk of dark time is night. Days and nights, darks and lights collect in purposeful, moody groups I know as seasons.

Spring. Summer. Fall. Winter. What large keepings of dark, light, time and space, purpose and change! I am in awe of the seasons bringing dark and light to touch my skin. They nourish my mind and spirit; they cultivate inside and outside spaces. I love the strong feel of earth underfoot. My human core needs the connection with the Earth. I long for the freedom of the space I know as sky. I lie in the grass beneath the ash trees in our yard—let my body and being become grounded as they tune to the earth and sky. Though I cannot see sky, I spread my arms, my wings. My senses reach for space and substance. Overhead, tree branches shift in the breeze. They dapple my skin with messages of coolness or heat or seasons changing. My mind and spirit take in the spaces around me where dark and light roam, where day, night and seasons happen. Then, smack dab in the middle of this connection blares the siren. It howls out its disturbing practice warning once each month throughout Minnesota's tornado season. Wow! Every urban reality crashes in on me. I remember where I am—safe—in my yard—and I choose to give thanks for this modern help and return to what's more natural.

I honor dark and light and seasons by knowing their truths and mysteries. I honor them with my own lore. Sometimes I describe season upon season as rolling like hoops. Mostly, I imagine dark and light as two frisking Labrador Retrievers. Picture this pair of labs named Dark and Light. Hear their collars jingling across the field. Hear them frolic, barking life into being with joy.

Memories of earlier seasons filter into the present. Possibilities of future seasons flavor my being and days. Past and future serve as cornerstones to my here-and-now living. Seasons extend my connections in time and space; they expand my certainty of belonging to all kinds of meanings and experience in this universe. In contrast, seasons also make me fully aware of nothingness and everything—space and time without defining, confining or measure. Sometimes dark or light patches of time feel like stepping stones. Sometimes daytime and dark feel like door mats before unimaginable doors open. I do not take dark and light, day, night and seasons for granted. I acknowledge them. My knowing dark and light, day or night and seasons can come in practical, serious or whimsical moments. In private and personal, shared or public, outdoor and indoor, social or political, rural or urban settings, each influences me. None is less valued than the other.

MY PHYSICAL WORLD

In my physical world, there is no sky;
But there is air and there is earth.
There are perceived, yet no visible stars;
But there is sun and there are clouds.
Summer sun packs heat.
And even I squint up at her glare.
I know there are clouds, for they block sun's warmth,
Shifting me as I move from warm to cold,
In their slow dance, big as buffaloes.
Clouds shear away echoes and shapes of sounds
As the shearer changes the looks of sheep by shearing their coats in spring.
Clouds bring dust or rain or snow.
I take in the shadows they bring to me.
In my physical world, there is no sky;
But there is a moon; there are seasons and tides.
Seasons come-rolling, go-rolling as hoops:
Spinning, slowing; spilling then sprawling.
Then, some universal hand
Sets them up, and sends them on.
I know there's a moon. I know there are tides,
For the moon pulls their brewing.
Stirring, then surging, they merge with sand.
I feel their froth. They poise, then turn:
Roaring, crushing, shooshing, hushing.
Rolling, pulling, pushing;
They rush and shove to get on shore;
They run to sea.
In my physical world, there is no sky;
But there is empty, yet meaningful, physical space.

Near, for me, in physical space
Is when I stand and speak on wide open prairies.
Each word, like a bone, speaks truth alone.
No echoes bring them home again.
Only air and scents and grasses touch me.
Far, for me, in physical space,
Is when dreams and my recollections rise.
Their voices call as sea gulls cry
Off canyon walls and oceans.
Deep, for me, will always be
To wonder at your workings,
Old undulating elephant-earth
Where I move along your margins.
I walk upon your skins;
I know your heart is thrumming.
In my physical world, there is no sky:
But there are created meanings and measures of time.
"Then," for me, as time circles on
Is all that is back, away or beyond.
All I remember, or dream may come.
Then, that which is known or dreamed or may be
Is machined and distilled into butterfly now.
There is nothing illusive here
In this fully evolved butterfly who is evolving still!
In my physical world, there is no sky;
But there is air and there is earth.
There is sun and there are clouds.
There is moon pulling tides.
There are seasons, space and time.
There are thens—
And,
There is the miracle, NOW!

Come, here's my hand. Step around to my off-dog side. There. That works. Gala's harnessed—ready to go. Take a literal walk through this year's seasons of dark and light with Gala, my dog guide, and me. We'll get metaphorical and symbolic later. Come. Step outside and turn in a joyful circle. Tip your face up. Be part of each day and night, dark and light time. Take in each season. Let them take you in. Find your own unique ways to give praise. Come, let's see what traveling together holds for us all. Need jackets? Water bottles? I have extras. Got a bus pass so that's covered. Got a cell phone if we need to call for information or assistance? Here, tuck some apples in your pockets. Wear good walking shoes and tie them in double bows. Where do you have to go to get good shoes, shoes that fit your feet well and keep you styling on all occasions? I go to a Schuler Shoestore which is within a short drive or a long walk. Ready? Well then, let's go.

Walk with us along the left edge of country roads, city streets and sidewalks, in what I claim as the "Jane Lane." In all kinds of weather, wait for—maybe miss—buses and appointments along with us. Crabby or peaceable? Your choice.

"Gala, forward. Atta way, girl." And what about safety? We'll be as safe as we can be by doing our level best in a world where there aren't any guarantees. There are days when we do everything right and still nothing works out in a predictable manner.

When Gala and I work, it is up to me to hold the day's route information in place in my head, assess and integrate changes, and hold us to our route. As we go, Gala counts on me for this. It is up to her to work each command I give. Once in a great while, I count on Gala to disregard a given command—this is what dog guide trainers and we handlers call intelligent disobedience. Then, I count on myself to honor her cues. She counts on me to go with her as she works. We count on one another. The result is a great one.

"Gala, forward," I say, and she doesn't move. I wonder why and focus my senses to pick up clues. No out-of-place aromas—no unusual sounds. I raise an exploring hand and find no protruding objects or overhanging branches. When I put an investigating foot out to see, I find an open construction hole with no barricades in place.

"Good girl. Hup (Get to work now.) Find a path around." She does, and as we go, we bask in confidence and satisfaction. We navigate all kinds of architectures, from auditoriums to state fair tents, from Grand Central and Port Authority platforms to boat docks—not always easily, but we get there. As we travel through our neighborhood, we work around permanent urban landmarks such as drop boxes, fire hydrants and buildings. Changing cues such as sirens, street cleaning, roadwork or construction site barriers also help orient us. We work with traffic, but I often wonder if I know enough about a crossing as I tell Gala to head into it. We encounter people, but doing what and how close to us? What do the voices and words I hear tell me? Nothing? Much? What will my handling strategies be: skilled and practical, thoughtful or intuitive? BlindSight, direct me to coping confidence.

Sometimes there are problems. On one occasion a vehicle slowed beside me. A male voice called, "Say miss…"

Without moving closer, I paused, responded, "How can I help you?"

I expected a request for directions. I got an explicit, filthy, sex proposition instead. Part of my sluggish mind kept grabbing onto direction asking and giving — that's what should be happening. I turned away from the voice and paid strict attention to my dog and our work. "Hup! Atta girl"

As we travel through urban and suburban settings, I anticipate much and take most of it in stride. I expect buses, trucks, cars, drop boxes for mail, fire hydrants and utility poles. I find vehicles parked in all kinds of ways: poking out over sidewalks, blocking driveways, double parked, angled to curbs or parked in tight parallells. I find children's bikes and other toys, garbage bags, cans, hordes of recycling containers, dead critters (cats, raccoon, rabbit, squirrel, occasional snakes and skunk are common), live critters (loose dogs are the most prevalent regardless of leash laws), and all kinds of objects and unwrapped (grab-it-if-you-can) food to distract my dog from work. Don't forget winter ice hillocks or tree-root-initiated cracks; there are tar and gravel road-repair smears to get around or through. They must be circumnavigated just the same. Particular precaution is necessary in rural settings where farm dogs must be freed to do their jobs.

Zoo trips can be droll; many critters come close, curious about who's come to visit. Gala does not do amusement park rides or water slides with me. Other event settings, particularly the American Kennel Club (AKC) and the North American Hunt Retriever Association (NAHRA) hunt tests we frequent, bring on other challenges. Gala's instinct: "I know I can do that! My gene pool says so and every fiber in me says go show them!" v.s. Gala's training: "Okay okay! I'll guide your butt around the dogs and decoys, past the ponds, the pigeons and ducks." Initially, Gala did not like the afternoon I spent on the high ropes course at Presbyterian Clearwater Forest. Worried puts it mildly. Caring hands and voices smoothed down her anxieties. Then she looked up at me, got it that she didn't need to help, and settled into her comfortable curl to watch and wait.

Whether working with my dog or a sighted guide, I always keep tabs on that great environmental experience, our Minnesota weather. How much? Which kinds? The consequence of weather changes significantly impact how, when, where, and whether or not we travel. The quality of the air, the feels and smells of the ground, and the sounds around us are just a few of my constant considerations.

When traveling, my trusty kinesthetic and sensory (especially auditory) systems provide vital information. These systems quickly alert me to changes before my mind makes sense of them. Thus on any normal travel day, without a lot of conscious thought, skin automatically judges temperatures, feet catalogue route textures. Why aren't there sidewalks here? How did I mess up my route? Muscles stretch on the levels, push up hills and tell me about it. My scent gathering and naming processes are always at work. I listen for changing silences and sounds.

COMING SPRING

One grand old fable tells a great old wager
Between the wind and the sun.
It's the annual war between winter and spring.
Which of us can coax those humans to take off their coats?
One tugs and tussles, snatches, huffs!
The other warms and warms.
Thirty-one rounds they struggled through
Before Spring gets the title.
And suddenly, today I hear
A cardinal's slow-going, two-toned whistle.
Yoo-hoo. Dee dah. High. Low.
I tip my head from side to side in sync.
That song tips seasons and my being.
Tips the solstice, shifts earth's axis.
Changes lighting; shifts my soul
Teeter-totters everything from winter into spring.
One moment feels pansy petal fragile.
The next is buttercup bold.
One dawn shivers me down to my bones with cold
While another,
Gray-quiet, kitten belly soft;
Stills my hands.
Then, tulips and crocus point the way
While stove black crows float.
In the wetland woods across the street,
Peepers and their old frog folks
Open their jar-like mouths and their cave like throats
And, like green mechanics with monkey wrench voices

Ratchet tight sounds up bamboo scales.
Out of harness now,
My dog guide Gala stands
At ease—at hand—right here beside me.
Tail waving small, sure circles of joy
That keep time with timelessness.
We all are short-timers here
With a long time to be gone.
We take in; give back all we can
Let ourselves suspend on hold
So full of what is possible.
We hang, in the moment, like hammocks between
Stark realities of frost
And simmering, summer pots.

Spring sweats off my winter clothing. She pulls zippers, nudges buttons open, rolls up the sleeves of my flannel shirt. She slips through my hair, down my collar, up my jeans, mucks my boots, soaks my socks. She paints each bare toenail with sunshine, scrapes away necessary winter layers and cracks through my protective husk. Stiff joints are heated and oiled to reach far and often; my blood is stirred. My mind and spirit breathe slow and deep: my heart makes up songs, and my mouth sings them in rhythm to our motion. She, this sunrise season, affects me to my core with butter soft warmth in her mellow, but persistent light.

Returned spring geese and robins rouse Gala and me. Now, all my being wants action more than rest. Gala, too, samples spring with the flick of her tongue. I feel earth's vibrant, thrumming heartbeats pulsing in me. Train sounds muffle as the grass grows and the leaves come. Their calls to journey do not attract me now. Growing right here is much more interesting. I brush out Gala's winter fur and carefully store the togs that have served me so well: the hat-scarf combo that warms my ears and protects my face without muffling sounds or blocking my sense of nearby objects; my red mittens and the shooting gloves whose fingers pull on and off easily for better dog-harness handling; the light weight down jacket that warms me without being a heavy hindrance to free movement; the supple boots that help me feel and hold to the ground under tricky winter surfaces.

Gala and I walk gritty streets and meander the sidewalks. We stop longer than usual at the corners just so I can listen and dream hilarious dreams. It's the only time I can let my mind wander. We step with splashes into muddy puddles and smell the ground's moist scent. We walk south, houses and yards on my left. My nose smells wood smoke, fabric softener, animal waste, oil-based paint, Oscar de la Renta perfume (nice), and human fear (keep forward facing and moving. But but but??? Where's that coming from?). This spring morning we're part of the company of creation where every kind of language is spoken.

Gala's pleased motion, bird's songs and mine, still things, even the traffic and whatever fear I noticed, are all part of this spring day.

Three busy lanes of north/south traffic paralleling us on the right and three lanes of perpendicular traffic crossing just ahead. I'll cross south over Medicine Lake Road, turn right (west) and cross Winnetka Avenue North. I wait to hear the first car in the middle lane reach the midpoint before we go.

We arrive at our first curb, step up smartly, out of the busy traffic. I say with words and a hand signal, "Gala, forward. Gala, right. Good girl."

We make the crossing and turn south on the west side of the street. What's this? Vehicles moving fast—honking—on both sides of me. Oh, shit, we are on the traffic median. My route-holding mind has dangerously goofed. Now what? Don't duck; don't scrunch your shoulders. Face forward. Talk to your dog; calmly, quietly, with serious purpose in your voice, Jane—keep her working. Keep yourself working. Is it safe to finish the crossing now? Good. "Gala, forward." Phew! That mess is behind us. That's a fate-tester for the Guinness book of dog guide world records. We stop. I breathe deep. Unbuckle Gala's harness and pull it off. Praise her for superb work. We rest while I rub her down and we talk. I/we get ready to go again.

Many folks say it takes real courage for humans to place their lives in the care of their dogs. Without hesitation, I say that from my dog guide's perspective, it takes courage to work with me. "There now. Atta girl, Gala. Cross at the first street beyond the tracks. Good job."

Walking home while cool spring dark teases my senses and evening birds call are miracles whose time comes in spring. Open, soften, tune to her, chase away the hard closed winter by living steady and well. I feel the pull of the full moon's light or is this the power of the dark moon's attraction? My hands reach up and open. The rest of me follows their lead. Spring dark gives me mysteries to hold. They flow like new music. Spring's starlight plays over me, touches me in filigree. Spring absorbs my being. She invites and blesses all my ways of growing. For me, choosing to grow comes in spring. Spring, come often throughout my life. Please, accept my humble thanks.

As Mary and I were growing up, Mom taught at Lewis and Clark College and then worked as the Dean of Students there. One of the great experiences we had was experiencing this beautiful college campus, its staff, students and activities. They were integral parts of our everyday family and lives. We never took them—especially our luxurious poolside summer days—for granted.

POOL SIDES

Mary made the tuna fish
While I talked on the phone.
We grabbed our suits wrapped up in towels
And, sometimes enemies, today good pals,
Walked the two mile trail uphill to school
For a long summer day spent at the pool.

SUMMER MINNESOTA STORM

When the wind blows me and my dog around,
My hat, hair, pack straps and jacket sleeves
Flap and snap like flags.
And the rain
Comes and comes,
Comes and comes and comes.
Some wind-driven rain
Slices and digs into me like grapefruit spoons.
Full, plump, juicy-ripe drops
Splash against my back like grapefruit chunks.
They sluice over my hat—slant into my eyes;
Slur into my ears—barge into my mouth;
Parade along my arms—beat tattoos against my hands;
And roll down my legs to drum on my shoes.
Soon, the wind slows and stops.
Then rain
Comes and comes,
comes and slows; comes and slows—and slows.
Each heaping drop is a tablespoon brimming,
Fat and full as a nursing breast.
I am hungry—I need this rain.
Now, it is a Minnesota "Fishing Rain."
Silver rain dances on Gala, my golden girl.
Since she is harnessed and working,
She merely flicks it with her tongue.
But I turn my face up—I wide-open my mouth to it.
When Gala gives her mighty, water shucking shake,
All the crawling worms might wonder,
"What kind of a golden, four-legged storm
Can slap this much rain down on us?"
Soaking wet, we walk along—blown by the wind and filled with its spirit.

Summer is the queen of let's get-the-job-done. More like the queen of forced marches, really. "Grow! Grow! Grow," is her push push pushing cadence call. Where is the same gentle sunshine I turned to, soaked in and slow-danced with during spring? The intense summer light and hurry-pace make me feel like scorched fried eggs. I'll just stand here—take some personal dog days. Root deep if summer's going to push hard to make me grow. Ugh, street tar and oil coat my shoes and Gala's paws with gooey stink. That's what we get for standing still. No thrumming earth beats now. How does this pure yellow energy of heat and light and sound so readily singe away each layer between my skin and core? Do I have a core worth hearing—finding—being? Will it grow so much I'll burst like a milkweed pod?

One well-aimed golden ray of heated energy gently caresses my forehead, slips down to the tip of my nose, invades my heart, stuns my mind. It reminds me that summer is doing what she does best—pushing! Making me risk hurrying. Ah, hurrying—a leap of faith forward today or yet another struggle to outwit fear? Guess I won't know until I take the step, will I? Gala's golden hackles rise to accompany my summer-alert status. She doesn't growl; she does not protectively stand in front of me across my body. She stands intently by, waiting and ready to work as needed through the busy, buzzing yellow angst of summer.

For this part of today's traveling, the sun slants over my right shoulder now. Lucky to have it today. Here come gusty wind and slapping rain again. If you don't like the weather in Minnesota, just wait a minute. No rain gear with me. Not good preparation. Gala, can I borrow your coat? Wind and rain bluster into my hair and clothes, bump into my skin, block traffic sounds. Hear the absence of rain? We must be under a footbridge or overpass. Keep going, cross the tracks. Turn left before crossing the next street. Near lane can turn right on red, middle lane gets an advance start. Listen for the parallel middle lane to get a quarter way through the intersection and go with it. Walk east...no sidewalks there. Three blocks of mud, green grass or dusty-dry ground, depending on the day. And so goes my travel log. I pull myself together, wring out my mind, my senses and my sleeves; call upon all my resources to regroup. Step, trust. Step, focus. Step and keep on keeping on.

Some summer nighttime forces hammer down, impose dark on dark, slash what lives by day with storms. Summer, how did you become such a fierce auntie to gentle spring's cricketing darks and lights? How could spring need you? How is it that what grows because of you is so fine?

FLY-AWAY

Full of Spring and Summer doings
Fall flies to Winter as geese fly south.
Autumn is eager and ready to go.
She is the smell when pies start burning.
Autumn earth and sky colors are
The so browns;
The deep golds or brilliant yellows; the burnt oranges or too reds;
And the hard-yearning blues.
What winter alchemy works them
Into powder white or pewter gray; stove black and stunning silver?
Winter's first touch appeals to me
Like the first duck call on opening day.
Winter nuzzles my hand like a dog nosing it for treats.
I gladly accept and offer myself.
I have been bagged.

Easy fall light heats me to the bone. Her sundown mysteries turn my soul to butterscotch. The hard summer pace eases. There is more giving among earth and sky, the world and me; I experience some blessed sense of collaboration. I feel ripe and full to match autumn's fullness. What gifts. With kind persistence, fall slants her delicious knowing into my fullness—makes me restless again—for change? Turn inward now. Rest. You cannot stay full of summer's natural energy, light and life. You can keep her power and memory with you. Gala touches her nose to my hand, presses her shoulder against my thigh. "I'm here, too."

We walk miles in this transition time. How we love walking on bike paths or kicking leaves along tree-lined country roads. "Fall," I softly sing the old-time song line, "you have such a short time to be here; such a long time to be gone." Autumn's a wise, old woman, shooshing about. She melts my fearsome fight, makes me long for rest. Gives me all she can before she goes. We lean against the fence, hunker down on the porch steps, sit on the grass in a pool of golden ripeness shot through with winter. Fall and I take each other's measure. She shrinks my physical self and like a ripe and ready nut, she blankets my memories of a full year with her hard shell. I feel compact. Spare. Golden-furred Gala curls down beside me tightly like a coiled spring. Touching her brings me to wondering tears. Can this year's experiences, strung together like beads, become next year's basis for new experiences or achievements? Might this year's memories, small as mustard seeds, spark life a-growing yet again? The geese call their g-o-i-n-g and train whistles sound their sharp, clear imperatives in bare-branched spaces. Time and seasons will tell.

AFTER THAWS

We have just come off a thawing-time.
—Down to zero once more,
Repeatedly, the currents of wind rise and fall;
They pirouette softly, or subside into pockets of stillness;
Drive straight on through me like a well struck golf ball.
They buffet me as if they were disoriented, newly blinded folks
Determinedly getting through the world.
But there is no snow yet.
For days
Radio stations have given every version of
Brewing, prowling, coming or dying storms.
But there is still no snow.
Then, throughout one night, it flurried;
not the predicted foot, nor eight nor six nor even two inches,
We got just enough snow
To get a mile of meaning and a world of work!
It was just enough snow
To force on boots, track up floors,
And blot out pointers to spring.
And there is such a hush all over the world.
It is clean and deep and good and right.
It is so quiet. Can it be trusted?
Sometimes, after love-making, it is like this, too.

Stunning winter dark and light crackle like an old crone's bones before a fire; they hiss and simmer like a hot spring. She, this two-fold witch of deception, holds me still, protects me from herself with herself. Her shadows, like pelts, cover me but without any warmth. Fierce, two-in-one sisters, winter dark and winter light join to insist, "Child, rest". How can there be any comfort in that? My house, this body I know, soldiers on, keeps a stiff, architectural upper lip. How could it not, with reinforcing ice, snow and wind at work? Some of winter's force (is this the dark sister?) presses her chalk board flatness against me. I shiver and hunch down. More winter force (the light sister?) hits me with the cold, glaring light of bone china. My whole body squints. Winter's first snowflake pings against my cheek with poignant clarity and brilliant cold. I absorb her. Is this snowflake a point of light? like the star in the east that caught and held the world in awe so long ago?

Gala lifts her muzzle to test winter's scents. Picks up her paws one by one. "Go? Stay? My paws are cold. Choose."

"Hmmm. Shall I slip on your boots, girl?" The hard-packed frozen and still, ice-coated, snow-blanketed, wind-swept geography stuns our work. Clouds, like the fat, gray, hard under-bellies of ships, full of the possibility of coming snow, settle down upon our heads.

"Gala, hup left. Good girl. Get that left curb." She trots to it before I finish speaking. Reaching to confirm it with the touch of my booted foot, I find that she's as tight into it as the banked snow allows. Gala confidently moves forward for a long way, then makes a considering stop. Did we miss that sneaky curb cut corner? Are we in the middle of the street? My route-storing mind tells me what is too snow covered for my feet to confirm. We're at the corner. My brave, yet timid heart asks, which opportunity is this, Jane? Chance to praise good work or ask for more clarity? I choose to praise Gala with lavish words and pats for making the stop she knows is beneath there somewhere—right there—and we plow on through. Only when I walk with a sighted guide do I dare to think about traveling on automatic pilot.

Beyond all this, do you think something is vitally limited, missing and wrong in these finite pictures of Jane and Gala traveling through dark, light, and seasons? Years of living blind and walking in the world tell me there is. This culture in which I live says that, whether outside or inside us, dark and light are value-laden, powerful opposites. Living blind offers me a larger, new understanding.

I choose not to confine my understandings of sunlight and energy, waking and growth, to day. I do not limit dark and rest to night. Dark and light are not opposites for me, they are different aspects of, or faces on the same life-giving energy. Light, as I live it, is larger than daytime light. There is darktime light as well. Dark, as I live it, is larger than nighttime dark. There is daytime dark, also. I entreat you, let dark and light as you know them take wing. Along with me let natural dark and light be neutral; let each be positive, and altogether new. Let them be worth exploring and traveling through in more than one way. For me, dark or light exist any time, anywhere. Often, for me, they exist together in a remarkable blend.

Just as living blind has created BlindSight for me, now it produces this rich, new fusion of dark and light, a phenomenal hybrid I have named DarkLight or LightDark. Either works. As such, this fusion is an all encompassing experience which provides a quiet, safe, honest inner space for barrier-free outer and inner life. Because I can pay less attention to whether or not it is physical day or night, whenever I am awake, I am free and ready to be and do on high alert. Yes, I've had to learn not to disturb others if it is physical night.

This Darklight personal space has shape. It is like a fire ring or a clearing. Here, in this frank coming together, my inside fists unclench, personal walls break down. This place is exquisitely and exclusively mine. It is a treasured retreat from all the people who thrive by pigeonholing me or deciding what's appropriate for my life without checking with me first. Nobody enters this DarkLight place but me and mine. There's room—all kinds of room—for all of me. No part is pressed down or turned away here. All parts have freedom of movement; I am the only referee. When pieces of who I am enter, they gain light within light, space within space, time inside time. When I come away from this space, I bring with me truer senses of myself and what I want for my life. I am clearer about what actions to take.

In this personal place, there may not always be answers, but there is time and space for process, and process is often answer enough. What gifts of peace and strength. There is time to remember, to dream and know. Time to contend with, understand and accept every facet. Time to sort through issues I face; let the unresolvable sit still. Here in LightDark, awareness and dreams, certainties and fears, hungers, needs, or wishes can speak. Here, my life imperatives also join the congregation of contributors. Do and feel, speak and write, work and play. Help yourself and help others. Let others help you. Do not always take action. Give yourself time to be. And, do not always take yourself so seriously.

Finally, the facts of my life enter and make themselves comfortable here in this personal clearing. I am my age, class, color, disability and sexual identity. Welcome home, evolving ideas about how I fit into life and my culture, awareness of personal geography, deepening faith walk and struggles with institutionalized religion.

When all my pieces hold forth and contend toward truth and equity, I am energized. If it all gets too serious and I get too earnest; if the mob's hubbub gets too contentious and I grow weary or lose my temper; and, in order to live with it all, I need them to stand down some, I imagine the lot into a herd of old cows, bells clanking as they lope toward the quiet haven of the DarkLight barn, their feed troughs and rest.

LightDark is the mixing and integrating of all my life. Thank you, DarkLight. You give me time and space in which to examine my culture-imposed perceptions of personal strangeness. Sometimes this strangeness makes blindness out to be exotic—why do you wonder what it's like to make love to a blind person? At other times, this weirdness gets me viewed as a stigma—remember the Rorschach test, a single blot on an otherwise perfectly clean and clear page, in my case, the double whammy of two blind eyes in an otherwise perfectly normal face? This is a superb illustration of how many perceive and remember my blindness.

BlindSight, give me new knowing for my life. DarkLight, please do your work in my spirit. Push me, carry me, or teach me to walk, but don't leave me with the sense that I am an extreme stranger here. BlindSight and DarkLight, please, create for me conversations with others and paths that I can trust in this part of the journey. I want to connect with live, spirit communities in and beyond this personal world I hold dear. DarkLight, what changes are you allowing to happen now? I feel as if more space—new space—is pushing to open up in me. Will this space empty or fill me, will I inhabit it? Will it inhabit me; or will we dwell together?

Once I trusted myself to welcome new life into my existing inner life, she came. By her actions, she let me know that her name was Transforming Grace—T-Grace or TG for short. She moved into my DarkLight space, convinced my timid heart toward bravery so that I dared to consider naming this inner space my Church-within-me spot. Sits right down in the middle of this human sack of skin and bones, muscle and blood, heart and mind, and goes to work—convinces me that, whether deficient or sufficient by my own or other human measures, whether weak or strong, I am "fearfully, wonderfully made". Entreats me to accept that every part of me is a gemstone in a mine, and a shining star in a constellation. She gently admonishes or rebukes attitudes of mine; clears away debris and gets me going again. Takes hold of the old familiar me. Plainly shows me that sometimes you just can't shape new life by reworking the present with the past—that's like refinishing old furniture. It's still old stuff! You must infuse new, as yet unwritten, unspoken future into being. When gentleness isn't getting the job done, T-Grace gets militant with me. Grabs my cynical mind and skeptical spirit and, whenever they turn me away, by her exemplary teaching, she turns them toward discernment and trust, creativity and productivity, compassion, joy and peace again.

I could not have faith without the help of Grace. This savvy force rolls up her sleeves and works in me. She works on my behalf. She takes on—lets me take on—life's adversities and challenges. She is no less regal or earthy because she fits in and around me. Sometimes T-Grace and I fit like nesting bowls. In some situations, I feel us balanced as if she is a gift of books upon my head or amazing weights set upon my outstretched hands. Now and then TG and I fit together like casserole layers with a variety of tastes or the dense rich fusion of homemade chocolate pudding. When I feel like an insignificant lump of clay, Transforming Grace builds me up or strips away excess so that I can be the best there is for me to be at the time. Then, I walk tall and sure. Amazing Grace gives me truths and she gives me jobs to do. She can call something forth in me that resonates like a bell. This is what transformation acts like in me and my life. It creates an extraordinary ordinary me. What joy! She convinces me to give in this world rather than to withhold. She directs me to tasks. The life-giving, creative task to which Grace harnesses me is: "Take heed to the ministry that thou has been given that thou fulfill it." (Col. 4:17)

Valliant Grace does more than connect me to valuable inner space, living well and jobs to do. She connects me to believing without seeing and she connects me to a Person who is much more than personality, whom I have come to realize is Everlasting Life. This believing without seeing—without visible evidential proofs—is what I call faith, walking with Grace. This is not religion per se, but living life as a faith walker; letting my finite humanity link to the sacred infinite where transformations by Grace can come. To believe in what none of us can physically see takes a special part, a spirit part of us all to start. I have come to call this higher, deeper, inner power and life force by many names. The first that come to mind are: Living God, Alive and The River of Life, enough and complete. Creator, Redeemer, Sustainer. Creator: because of whom, the one who receives and gives. Redeemer: the one in whom I find the ultimate, meaningful relationship. Sustainer: to whom I give thanks many times each day and who provides constant love. It's these understandings that prompt me to sing the Vineyard Press song, "I will make my plans, Lord, but you direct my steps."

Here's what I recently heard an old folk hymn written by Gordon Jenson say: "God is bigger than all my questions. God is bigger than anything…" Now that's MIGHTY BIG. For me the faith walking I do is not a cop out, not a crutch, not a crock. It is all about believing in hope. As a friend recently reminded, faith walking is a courageous inner awareness of and commitment to HOPE—Having Other Possibilities Exist. Hope, I confidently assert, is proof and consequence of Grace at work.

Living blind, thank you for bringing me face to face with BlindSight—the knowing that comes from accepting all of myself into being. BlindSight, thanks for opening me to DarkLight—the being that makes room for spirit knowing in me. DarkLight? You enhance my world. Thanks for doing what I could not do at first—you make room in me for transforming Grace to make emptiness full and fullness into a blank slate, ready for more. Because of you, I celebrate the many ways I have of looking at things. I value walking in the thousand worlds I know. LightDark touched with transformation Grace, thanks for your blessings. Thanks for teaching me that life is a being journey. Has living blind finished instructing me and my spirit about dark, light, day, night, seasons, LightDark and Grace yet? I don't think so. I hope I remain willing to learn and discover until life here on earth is done. Blindness is key; she is the lens that teaches the rest of me how to see. Living blind is the doorway through which my opinions and perspectives and all the pieces of my identity gladly step. I never leave her behind; she's never left me out. Am I finished walking through dark, light, seasons and DarkLight? No, not until I find ways to share this inner clearing with others. One way I imagine this sharing happening is the same way I experience my trout pool splashes. They ripple and circle then touch the pond shore. "Gala, let's go. Forward. Atta girl."

CHAPTER FOUR

Journey with Disability: A Cultural Challenge

Until I became an adult, I had absolutely no idea what culture and society were or that they had powers to affect perceptions of who I was as a person living with blindness. When I repeatedly ran into social, educational and employment barriers, I started asking questions. Who or what is behind this powerful thing called culture? How does culture work in my life to hold me back, put me down, keep me in place, categorize me, set me apart, push me forward or move with me? It became essential for me to grapple with cultural realities that had such power to control, curtail or free me.

My culture has often intentionally blurred the lines between disability and talent in order to minimize the consequences. For someone to experience the limits of being a poorly skilled typist is not the same as experiencing the limits to daily life function that a disability imposes. When someone unthinkingly says, "But everybody has some limits", I respond with, "You want to swap?" Then they get it. Right there in the details of my life is one arena in which I wage my struggles to reinvent cultural attitudes and actions toward disability and me. To do this, it became essential to grapple toward the beginnings of understanding about how my culture worked.

AFTER WE MEET

Maybe, just maybe, we can be friends
If you face me, accept me,
Get over yourself
And get on with welcoming me into your world.
I do this for you. Will you do it for me?
My physical blindness is a physical fact and a life-long experience,
The result of a long-ago accident.
I live with disability.
Do you understand? Do you feel safe?
I am not going away. I am not contagious.
You cannot catch it—catch me. It and I are not disease.
Here is an inescapable truth.
None of us can erase this fact.
In the twinkling of an eye, the snap of mind or twist of bones
(no talent is at work here to forever change your life)
You, too, may become disabled.
If you say to me once, "I'm so sorry this happened."
I mourn with you. I welcome care.
"Sorry" twice unnerves me.
"Sorry" again comes ripe with pity.
"Sorry" more speaks guilt!

My body houses all the same parts and systems as your bodies. The one small, irrefutable, physical difference: my eyes do not see—I am legally blind. Traditionally, my culture has described me as sightless—handicapped—visually impaired. Further, it traditionally has demonstrated its lack of inclusiveness by separating some services for able bodied and disabled individuals. Small differences, you say? No, I carefully respond. If my eyes, their physical blindness and the separation I have often experienced were as big as the baggage I've sometimes carried, they'd be big as elephants.

Let's first explore the definitions and experiences of legal blindness, culture, and society as they have evolved in my life.

My working definition of legal blindness is that my physical eyes see nothing. Light, dark and colors are absent from my life experience now. I am totally blind. Seeing is gone. I cannot see the look of you, whether or not you're pretty or ugly or how you are dressed. My eyes do not tell me what age, class, color, or gender you may be. They do not give me information about where you live or what kind of car you drive. I see none of the clues or cues about who you are. But, yes, I can learn about you by asking questions and listening. Similarly, you can learn about me. Perhaps you are puzzled about what it means to see nothing. Try this exercise on for size. Close your eyes. Make loose fists. Point them toward something or somebody you know is nearby. Hold onto this pose as you gather impressions. Now, answer these questions: What do your fists see? Do they see black, fuzziness, objects or people imprints? Anything? You're correct. Fists see nothing.

United States law declares that people are legally blind when, under specified lighting conditions, their best eye acuity is less than 20/200 with best correction, or that their field loss (what they see to the sides) restricts their vision to less than twenty degrees.

The Americans with Disabilities Act of 1990 says that disabilities are "mental or physical impairment substantially limiting one or more of a person's major life activities such as breathing, seeing, hearing, walking, thinking and a host of other hidden, and nonetheless vital functions".

My working definition of culture is as follows: Culture is everything that we say or do and the evolving reasons and rules why. Its effects infiltrate, surround and move with all of us, no matter where we are. Society, according to Jane, includes all the individuals and evolving groups who live within our borders. Many of our ancestors immigrated here (mine did—their stories stay with me today), found ways to learn and produce success for themselves and their families. Others have always lived here. Marilyn Frye, a sociologist, compares our culture to the vertical, rigid wires of a bird cage: "It is only when you step back, stop looking at the wires one by one, microscopically, and take a macroscopic view of the whole cage, that you can see why the bird (an individual or group) does not go anywhere..... It is perfectly obvious that the bird is surrounded by a network of systematically related barriers, no one of which would be the least hindrance to its flight, but which, by their relations to each other, are as confining as the solid walls of a dungeon."

In contrast to the immobilization of Frye's birdcage, I initially experienced culture in two ways. First, as a youngster, I experienced culture as a challenging swimming pool whose sides I had to push off against; whose waters I had to learn to swim in, through, then climb out of to resolve any problem. But, and far more powerfully, I experienced my culture as if it were the traveling ball in which a hamster safely, freely, eagerly rolls about.

Culture is always with me. Fluent and fluid. Moving with me just enough to make me mostly comfortable with and tolerant of it.

From my beginnings, I accepted walking as more than a life pleasure. It was an essential mode of travel for me. I believed I could meet challenges of knowing routes, using public transportation and arranging carpools. My family's "go, girls" attitudes and practices made all of this so.

As I grew and traveled farther from home, as problems surfaced, my family and I would handle them one by one, then dismiss them with "Everybody has some problems to face in life, right?" It didn't occur to me then, as it does now, that my personal freedoms are contained and curtailed by culturally defined and accepted barriers.

I now know that all those individual episodes have collective power and teaching in my life. Some examples of institutionalized cultural power include: special schools for the blind, isolating folks with disabilities into their own social support networks and clubs, institutionalized employments such as broom making, chair caning and piano tuning, together with institutionalized housing or work settings such as asylums, closed workshops or vending industries for the blind. When these segregations occur, the learning, the work and the social connections get devalued by the experience. Our country's serious lack of public transportation networks that would enable any non-driver to connect to all the strands of his or her life creates significant and multiple barriers for blind travelers.

I first began to think of the problems I ran into as cultural phenomena when I reached adulthood. I encountered transportation barriers such as, "Nobody's available to drive you." "No buses go there." "You can't walk home that late at night." "You'll just have to wait." Or social barriers such as, "Why would you be wanting to shop here, at New York's Bergdorf Goodman?" To me, these episodes are no longer ignorable flukes. They are the consequences of attitudes our culture engenders—access for all isn't a given, it's a privilege.

Culture is not a neutral, inclusive foundation on which we all stand. I wish it were. Whether or not we immigrated to the United States or were born here, this culture is a permanent collection of shared history. We are represented by and responsible for its past and present, whether or not we participated directly in all of its acts.

For me, there are tensions between historical perspectives and current perceptions. Yes, I cherish and honor journeys that brought many of us, for whatever reasons, from elsewhere in the world to citizenship here. I deplore the historical experiences and journeys that some United States citizens have forced upon others: people with disabilities, gay or lesbian individuals, American Indians and African Blacks, to cite a few.

Americans boldly, patriotically speak of welcome and freedom for all. In truth, our culture comes with powerfully spoken and unspoken rules about whom the "all" includes. Our democracy, however, comes with the stipulation that until people push our legal process to change the rules, our political decision makers will enforce rules that merely maintain the status quo—theirs, of course.

As human beings, we begin life with a wide array of physical characteristics, genetically determined behaviors and innate talents. This culture we share assigns positive/negative worth to individual attributes. The range of what is acceptable is fairly narrow. I call these value-laden differences "markers". In addition, culture directly and indirectly extends these powerful values to certain groups and experiences, e.g., marriages, families, educations, religions, our work, and oh, yes, our color and our sexual orientation.

Marilyn Frye described these and other markers as the wires that comprise her birdcage. Consciously or unconsciously, we all respond to these markers. When this response is strong and exclusive, it is a bias—it becomes a judgement.

It is difficult to become aware of and neutral about cultural markers without re-education. I know this first-hand. We all have complex personal identities which situate themselves along value-laden continuums of age, class, color, disability, economics, education, employment, personal geography, gender, looks, religion, and sexual orientation. My self portrait's fixed permanent markers include white, heterosexual, disabled, and female, while some of my evolving identity pieces include economics—more of us than you may realize are just a job away from working poor or poverty level—education, employment, looks, personal geography, and so on.

When I taught in a child care center, I discovered that the impact of these cultural markers on the children was compelling. They could affect even the well established areas of conventional early childhood theory and practice: cognitive, motor/physical, sensory, social/emotional, and moral/ethical. I struggled to deal with the confusion caused by many of my students' ever-changing and extended family shapes, their mobility and varying housing situations. I, too, needed to be re-educated. Over time and with help, I adjusted my expectations and teaching style to understand, include and respect these differences. I coped, yet not always willingly or well.

Now, here's what personal geography means to me and how it exerts power in my life. Personal geography is where you live, and how these locations broaden or curtail your day-to-day existence. Until age eighteen, I'd lived in Portland, Oregon, in urban or suburban (not rural) single-family dwellings with fairly consistent homogenous groups of people. I took personal space and privacy for granted. I could freely walk down our paved driveway, down the Carey Lane hill, across Macadam Boulevard, and stand beside the Willamette River. One early spring afternoon during my teen years, I stood on the river bank, realized that, river-like, I could travel to the sea, and unlike the river I could travel in many ways and in more than one direction.

In contrast, during my Syracuse University years, I lived in dorms or in off-campus apartments in crowded inner city neighborhoods. Personal safety required me to lock my doors whether I was home or not, always let others know where I was going, and to travel in groups where possible. During the first fifteen years of our married life, we lived in a wide variety of settings. We worked at combining vocational skills with avocational concerns. We moved from ministry to ministry, and lived in a variety of housing from a rambler overlooking a lake to a fifth-wheel trailer. Sometimes we shared others' homes, and often we existed at below the poverty level. At the time, these were not significant hardships. Tom and I were young, healthy and chose to live so.

Today, physical geographies I encounter here in Minnesota have the power to connect me to memories of life experiences that happened years back and far from here. When I stand at the mid point of the Mississippi River footbridge between the University of Minnesota's East and West bank campuses and take in the water smells and sounds, I hear little activity from either busy campus. The smell immediately takes me back to the banks of the Willamette, where the quiet never failed to be a strong and personal moment during which I was "on hold" and reminded to "live well." I need these reminders.

Today, hearing children skip rope on playgrounds or city sidewalks is another strong geographical reference point for me. Immediately, I connect with what I learned during my own Portland, Oregon childhood. Then, I jumped rope on the hot summer-day sidewalk in front of my house. I got the footwork down. Poised on the balls of my feet, I'd jump jump jump when the rope came down to them. I practiced the arms. Swung the rope up from behind. Got it over my head, and then let gravity pull it down. Could I get gravity and my ropes to work together? I would have to if I wanted to accomplish rope-jumping in my world. One shining moment in time, my strong arms held my rope poised above my head. The strength, energy and control in my arms traveled down to my toes. I knew to wait. I knew I'd know just when to jump.

Now, when I walk on hot summer sidewalks or stand on my Minnesota footbridge, I remember that, en route to achieving large and complicated life tasks, smaller manageable parts can be parsed. I remember that I can I choose to wait until I know it is time to move. This is the compelling power place has on me and how I live my life. The smells of the Mississippi, and sounds of rope-skippers take me right back to those instructional moments in Oregon. These memories help me today. I believe that living blind has been instrumental in giving me this opportune permission to stop and let geography remind me to experience life more fully.

Since seeing is the premiere sense, without sight, I am a constant, distressing reminder to others within this culture that an able bodied person can become flawed, might have to live with loss. I exist with the feeling that living blind equates with inferior. Shame on you, culture of ours, for being constantly disturbed by any less-than-perfect body. Shame on you for telling me that, on a few significantly appealing plains, I am an accomplished contributor here, while on far too many others, I am of little or no worth.

Recently, for instance, I interviewed to fill a teaching assistant's position in the nearby school district where my work and education credentials are known and matched the job requirements. I was asked, "Would you be willing to take the job for a trial period so that we can see how it will work for you?"

I answered, "For sure, if all other applicants are doing so." The essential understanding that was not allowed to carry weight in this interview situation was that I was job qualified and could have been hired without the trial period.

I believe that our culture falsely believes several things about blindness:

1. Blindness is an incurable problem; therefore, blind individuals are problems.

2. Blindness is a gift. It elevates a person to a more god-like status. The blind person is compensated with special, extraordinary sensory acuities and perceptions. As long as see-ers believe that my life holds fulfilling, compensatory, special powers, they are freed from guilt or obligation—they don't have to insist on or participate in making the world a more accessible place for all.

3. Blindness is a punishment for the sins of our parents or retribution for sins we commit.

Today, activists for disability rights say disability is a shared social/political experience. Disabilities and the people who live with them aren't the problems–they do not have to "be fixed" in order to be worthwhile. Since some in our culture live with disabilities, we all must proactively learn to live with them. Society, with its inaccessibility on many levels, is the problem. It has to be fixed; we all must share in its fixing.

I fight against the culturally accepted, appalling and erroneous belief that blindness (and by extension any other disability) is synonymous with whole-person deficiency or incompetence. It grieves me when folks meddle with me, leave me little or no room for figuring out my own paths. They seem certain that seeing as they see is what counts, that sight-based decisions are the ones that matter. Thus, knowing in all the ways I do counts for less or not at all. And there we have a stalemate. At such times, I am so weary that my face, the center of my sensory kingdom, feels as if it will fall off. So much talk and work to do before we can share the playing field, the stage, the job, or the relationship as equals.

But cultural struggles of living blind do not stop here. Others often think that, because they'd miss seeing so much, I miss it all the time. Too often, well-intentioned folks feel duty-bound to tell me when my husband and children smile. Some have softly implied or whispered, even boldly suggested, that my blindness might even have been responsible for, say, our children's negative adolescent behavior. What unfounded, inaccurate and inappropriate correlations! I also do not like the uninformed benevolence shown in the following kind of situation. Coupled with a pat on the arm or shoulder, some able bodied speaker states, "We know what is best," or "We did it with your best interests in mind".

When the thought of living blind overwhelms others, they beg me to make their learning easier for them. This request often silences me. I fret that my silence will be interpreted as submissive acquiescence rather than as self-defense. I can't make it easier for others—I can, though, be an ally while they do their own work. I make an effort to provide pertinent information. When what is real is too hard, when I need respite, I have choices. I can take perspective-changing walks or talk with others. If possible, I don't come back until I'm ready.

I can—I do—find it essential to reach out for community. Gather with other disabled fighters to gain solace and make our points. Take on access struggles, negotiate through the maze of attitudinal barriers and other loopholes to reasonable accommodation. Though dismissed if we push, we do it anyway, understanding that it must be done. Some of us even learn to push while remaining gracious; we dig in, ask for what we need, and help others ask on their own and other's behalf.

My culture has a lot to say about the look of a person. Since I would never see this look, it was harder for me to create my own image, or to come to understand what my actions looked like to others. In childhood, I learned what we all looked like within the framework of, and from feedback from my family of nine. There were my twin sister and I who did not see, and seven who did— mother, father, grandmother, Eula Lee, two older brothers and half sister Anne. I learned through interacting with my family about myself and what I wore, and by listening to clothes-buying comments made especially during our annual school clothes shopping expeditions to JC Penneys with Mom.

Mommy said to me, " Janie, you look soft and pretty in light blue, fresh as strawberries in that pastel pink, cheery in sunshine yellow, bright in firecracker red, crisp and cool in that deep-secret green. People can't help but want you around when you dress nicely, pay attention and show that you care when others speak. Mary, that shade of green would look better as a solid than it does in that plaid. Let's switch that jumper."

Busy Jane investigated everything that everybody wore. While my hands ran along the pleasures of the pair of corduroy pants my brother was trying on, I'd say, "I love the feel of this corduroy. But do its long lines make your legs look longer?"

From Eula Lee, the amazing woman who helped raise us all: "Honey Girl, you look worried. Why?" And she stroked a firm hand across the creases in my forehead, confirming that she knew my mood, waiting until they smoothed and I talked.

From my older sister Anne: "Jane Livingston Turner, get that snotty look off your face. Everybody can tell exactly what you're thinking."

Learning to make my face a blank page was hard work, let me tell you. Some of us are just plain born to let it all hang out. In contrast, if my facial expression happened to be smooth, quiet or still, I'd likely hear somebody comment about that. "Yoo-hoo, anybody home in there?"

From my middle brother when I was in kindergarten: "Jane, you can't stand in the corner of the playground and lift your skirt to pull down your blouse! Nobody does that!"

Confused, I hotly replied, "But I was trying to get tidy before the bell rang!" Social protocols must be taught; embarrassment is learned.

"Mary," I'd begin just as she'd say, "Jane." We'd finish asking together, "What do you want to wear today?"

My oldest brother told me something wonderful one day. "Janie, for sure clothes can make a difference, but not as much as how you act. So if it ever gets to be a push comes to shove match, act right. You'll be fine."

I also learned about how people looked and whether or not our culture approved, through hours and hours of listening to talking books, reading braille, and hearing print read by members of my family and some mighty fine girlfriends. During TV shows and movies, I'd insist on knowing what was happening, to whom it happened and what they looked like. I'd poke the person next to me and hiss, "What's happening? They're being quiet." To this day, I can still feel the motion of our car and hear familiar voices describe our culture's carefully or carelessly scrawled graffiti as it rolled by on buses, trains or trucks; I can still hear them read, describe or comment about what's standing out on bridges and buildings and billboards. Then, there were the waiting rooms, reception areas and grocery store check-outs where sighted readers skimmed magazines out loud, introducing me to the looks that matter in this society.

What our culture has trouble with is that we are not all the same. We don't look alike nor do we see alike. One way or another, this culture we share seems determined to make physical see-ers of those of us who do not. I still feel frustrated every time see-ers assume they must give me sight-gathered input before I even ask. I'm often amused when I compare the solid information I gather to the information see-ers initially contribute. How do we blend what you see and I know into something mutually useful and helpful?

We are alike and different. I don't want to feel I have to change in order to make you comfortable with me. I find that the longer I wait before speaking, the faster situations shatter into what I call sight noise. Sight noise is when seeing alone calls the shots. Just as I hate whitewater noise (a psychological ploy for urban calm) when it happens outside natural waterways, I hate sight when it is all that is respected. Sight noise overwhelms. It distracts and scares me. It ambushes me, sabotages my abilities to assess or handle situations. It creates false distance between me and whatever else is really happening.

Our culture is not ready for me in many ways. Why does it act surprised when I step through its doors and request assistance? Everybody else does. Bank tellers, museum docents, athletic coaches, restaurant staffs scramble to do the right things that often turn out to be wrong. Shop owners quickly and often ask, "How did you get here? Is there anybody I can call to help you?" Are they afraid I'll break or steal things? And so what if I need information in alternative formats? On the first day of class I often learn that the print materials for a university course aren't available in accessible formats as requested from the professor immediately following registration months ago. Many, certainly not all, professors still tend to confuse providing accessible materials with getting out of work or their doing my work for me. Once I have information, it is my choice and my stand-alone work that determine how and whether or not I will succeed. And finally, why do some physicians still tend to insinuate or outright ask if the root of whatever problem has brought me in is blindness?

A PLACE ON A BUS

We, this mother/daughter pair,
She old; I blind,
Step up from New York City muck onto a bus.
We dropped in our fares and asked for transfers.
The machine poked them back like stuck out tongues.
Our bus pitched and jolted. It grew ripe and close.
Riders grew ominously silent or loud.
"Sit here. No, sit here."
Some grabbed to assist without asking me.
I resisted their pushing; I chose to stand.
My mother's arthritis slowed her steps.
Yet years of bus travel kept her hustling.
One seat came open.
She said, "Sit down. Don't make trouble."
My damned white cane speaks loudly.
I don't even get to defer to Mom's age.
I don't get to show Mom my loving or caring.
I do not get to treat my Mom with respect!
Even she knows they would not understand.
Rosa Parks—
Teach me to ride all my buses
As you rode that particular bus one day.
Let my weary resignation be one determined act
Whose unexpected ends include inevitable dignity
And access for all.

And what does living blind teach me about see-ers in our culture? From where I sit, seeing, an ability most of us were born with, is an amazing sensory gift. See-ers easily (feels almost too casual to me) scan panoramas, peruse art, probe minute details, skim whole books in hours, pin others up against walls with glares. You are visually available to one another; see yourselves acknowledged in one another's eyes, communicate silently, express caring and invite intimacy with glances or winks across crowded rooms. Before your steps carry you there, your eyes can dart ahead to assess situations. And what good fortune and fun for you curious see-ers, eyes can eavesdrop and downright snoop from far greater distances than I, a listener, usually can.

What has living blind taught me about cultural symbols? Art, dance, drama, film, literature, media and music often use dark, light and blindness as symbols or metaphors for life actions and meanings. These symbolic experiences within our culture exert profound influence upon individuals and groups. All aspects of life are touched!

Consider how often the words "dark" and "blind" are used as positive or negative metaphors. With some exceptions such as "rich, dark earth" or "black is beautiful", these words become symbolic of negative experience. None of the self-respecting Blinks I know (insider name for people who are blind) equate the phrase "fly blind" with foolish or careless, ignorant or unaware traveling. We, like other pilots, might "fly" according to instrument readings or intuitively, but not by the seats of our pants. When, I ask you, have "blind" passions or rages played out any differently than plain old passions or furies? When has "blind justice" ever supplied equal justice for all? Why not say exactly what you mean? "I sure didn't see", or in my case, "hear or suspect that was coming", instead of saying "It blind-sided me."

Blind can also imply living without inner light and life. If eyes are the "windows to the soul," what might eyes that don't see imply about their owners? Similarly, consider how light and seeing get used as positive symbols of individual worth and cultural prominence. With a few exceptions, such as the dehydrating, hot light of drought, or the incendiary heat and destructive light of atomic bombs, light and sight suggest positive attributes. Symbolic light and sight have many implicit and explicit things to say about dark and living blind. This discussion is not to deny the powerful use of language that is abstract, symbolic or metaphorical —far from it. I am a lover of literal and symbolic language. For me, communicating in language creates and sustains life. I do, however, hope to challenge the thoughtless use of language in speaking or writing. And what about politically correct language? I say, begin with whatever respectful words you have whenever opportunities arise; learn as you share in conversations with others; make your points, ask your questions and move on from there.

What has living blind taught me about bias toward sight as the premier sense and those who see as our culture's standard? From where I sit, this bias toward see-ers or lookers and what is seen gets see-ers and we no see 'ems into big trouble. See-ers are considered accurate, normal, sufficient, and right, unquestionably trusted and relied upon as the brightest and best. Non see-ers are considered second class, inferior. I have learned that I must not internalize any of my culture's negative attitudes toward blindness—they do not have to apply to me. Sight can preempt other senses in acuity, which I can live with, but not in cultural worth and power, which repels me.

Since when do any of us really get to vote for who does or doesn't get to see, anyway? Never. So this privilege that see-ers enjoy is unearned. I think many like it like that. Why? Because, this way, distance unquestionably exists between see-ers and those of us who cannot see.

Our culture organizes itself to meet the needs of see-ers. All information is available in print. All physical, social and political space is accessible to those who see. Other's information gathering systems are measured against seeing. What is seen pulls rank on what other senses know. Very often, sight gathered information ends arguments in discussions or situations with the declaration, "Well, I saw it, so it must be so." My plea, my culture-sharing sisters and brothers, is this: Even while this natural gift of seeing is yours, please let others' gifts and resources matter in your lives. Be mutually useful and helpful to one another; this shared work can heal our culture.

It will be a better society for all of us when one way of seeing becomes one of many ways to see; when different ways of seeing count as equally important contributors for the good of our society. When you see-ers are as genuinely curious about living blind as I, out of necessity, have had to become about seeing in order to survive among you; when my difference is thought of with less distortion, negativity and fear and your seeing is questioned more often; when people speak and make room for others by listening well; when we use silence to affirm rather than to betray or exploit ourselves or others; when human differences are welcomed and treasured as our finest resource and allowed to form, inform, and transform us all, then we shall be equal. Will we have to learn how? I believe we all must risk it. We must look at our history and accept how it has imprinted us. We must intentionally push away the distortion and negativity. We must make new history: we must trust that there is a new path we can walk together toward equality.

CHAPTER FIVE

Journey with Language: Communicating in Speaking and Writing

When I was young, I heard a narrative poem called, "Six Blind Men and the Elephant" by the nineteenth century American poet, John Godfrey Saxe. Based on a Hindu parable, it is a fable about being whole, but it used blindness as a vehicle. It disturbed me then. It distresses me today. It's hard enough to live with blindness as a fact. Forget the vehicle bit! Anyway, others found it humorous. I don't. I took it as a statement that if you're blind, you're limited, and you can't know wholeness. I wasn't going to let that idea take any kind of root in me and my life by reciting or memorizing this tale.

In it, six blind men gather around an elephant. Each man dares to touch only one segment of this huge, unusual mammal. Believing he's "seen" it all, each man projects a notion of the whole creature based on the limited information he has acquired. I remember thinking, "I'm only six and I already know that you can't do that! You're going to trip over your own fear. It happens to me when I think I know the whole route to somewhere and forget to ask." During the fable's revealing conversation, not one man among them became willing to admit that his own frame of reference might be small. Each was unwilling to change his own position, explore the portions "seen" by his compadres, or to inspect the whole beast before speaking of other particular parts.

I remember not wanting to be that kind of person, somebody who didn't choose to learn when they could have. How dumb is that? Their talk sounded pompous and I didn't like it. And I did not like them for their limited inquiry into the situation. I didn't want my blindness, or anything else about me, to be responsible for what I determined to be fear or ignorance.

But, unfortunately, (fortunately as it turns out) though I did not memorize the poem, this story affected me permanently anyhow. It made me utterly aware of the power of language to create, sustain or destroy people and their lives. After I heard that story, I started talking to myself: "I don't like those men. I bet they stink. They didn't want to learn."

I talked to others: "Do you like that story? Why?"

Next I had a few pretend conversations with the author of the story: "Did you like showing me such little-minded, scaredy-cat men?"

Talked to the six men: "You don't have to be afraid. It's a big animal with lots of parts, that's all."

I talked to the elephant: "I'd love to explore all of you. May I? I bet your heart sounds like a quiet drum."

I desperately wanted to know if and when people I knew were like the men in the story. And, I wanted to put space between them and me. So, I talked to myself again about myself. I began to name who I was and how I wanted to be.

From that six year old to today, how did I eventually accomplish this? I lived differently by learning to use all forms of language definitively, descriptively and accurately. I learned the difference between stating facts and telling stories to make them meaningful. Language can push people away from me; I can use it to bring them close. Language, I decided, was the only thing that could establish my being and give me a place in the world.

It could be trusted to shape and support, anchor and extend my living and learning.

During my early years, I discovered that all living things, human beings included, have inherent characteristics. Each one's batch of characteristics is their particular packet of personal information. Language and how we use it makes us distinct among living things. Only language users communicate beyond the information inherent in our natural characteristics. Only we who use language can carry on interior and exterior conversations. With language, I can consider who I am, what I do and what I look like, define and describe my surroundings or myself as if I were inside or outside my skin. Only by using language can I adequately express my needs and beliefs.

When I use language well, I am strong, plainly visible and true within myself and the world. Conversations bring me to genuine self-knowing when nothing else can. I discover personal truths as I converse within myself, speak out loud, talk with others, and then listen. A conversation within myself or with others helps me to discern what part blindness plays in any given situation. Such conversations help me gain perspective and give blindness appropriate space when needed.

My two favorite kinds of sentences are questions and declarations. Like any journalist, I've learned to gather information with questions. Then, if I follow through by listening as the conversation unfolds and ask more, I can keep on learning. "How did this happen? How does this work? How did you come to be here today?"

Declarative sentences are favorites because they state what is so. I know the powerful value of clear statements. "Its name is ________" —you fill it in. Or, "No, I cannot do that right now" —you name the action you will not do. I revel in using language to start connections and make meanings; language gives me pathways and bridges to projects and people. I can use language to gather information, gain skills, share with and know others, work and play, and create life. How is it that learning, getting around and along in the world, hinges upon language? How I use language establishes me as a viable, productive and contributing person on the world's playing fields. Viable? Yes. I can establish sure footholds and handholds among social groups within my culture. With language, I can create pathways through situations. Productive? Yes. I can use body language, spoken language and, with more regularity now, written language to communicate clearly. Contribute? Yes. I use language to help people and share myself with others. I use words to challenge people to pay attention to me. Ultimately, using language saves me from being squelched, dismissed or ignored by others. Honestly shared conversation insures that others cannot belittle, dismiss, or ignore me. Most importantly, honest conversations can free me from consciously or unconsciously held assumptions. In such conversations, opportunities open for the questioner to actually hear and respond to a speaker's beliefs rather than for the questioner to presume that he/she already knows what is going to be said. Sometimes, I ask questions for which I cannot find answers. When I feel stalled or uncertain, I've learned to wait, start again, or reshape the question until I get somewhere.

Asking a question or being asked one is how my learning usually begins. I listen, compare answers about what others see and I know. I ask, "How do the colors and mood in that painting speak to you? What construction feature of this drum causes it to make such a deep, resonant sound? How do the conductor's hands tell the orchestra so much? Will you describe that crane operator, that building imploding, that barge, the way Rene Fleming stands when she sings? How did you arrive at those ideas or conclusions?" And finally, questions from all comers, whether I like them or not, prompt me to face myself and risk discovering whether or not my voice and words could speak in writing. Here, then, is the fifty-plus-year-long account of my journey toward communicating in speaking and writing. It develops and reflects how I learned and still learn, what I think and how I feel toward contributing in the world.

When I began learning to write, I thought it would be easy since I already loved what I knew first-hand about body language, spoken language and what I called insider language. Wasn't writing just spoken language put down on paper?

I knew that body language included all the ways bodies could communicate. My body makes sounds, moves or keeps still. I knew that people could let their faces express feelings or keep their faces blank. Early on, I knew about all this because it happened to me; my family, Mom especially, told me what she saw happening. I knew that everything my body and face did communicated as much or more than my voice sounds or words could. Knew that people interpreted the same actions and expressions differently, but they didn't often question their interpretations. Why not? Because seeing motion, gesture or facial expression sets see-ers up to presume they interpret the message accurately.

As I grew, I noticed body language at work in my conversations, the stories I told, and the books I read; it was there when others were speaking and singing, story-telling or reading out loud. It only took backing my words with wrong actions once to decide it wouldn't work for me. "I love you Mommy" accompanied with a big push didn't go over well and it confused my message.

Spoken language included every way people used voice sounds, words or silence to communicate. Talk has always enchanted me; I loved hearing people talk, even in other languages whose words were incomprehensible but whose sounds weren't. Incomprehensible? I never let that hold me back from imagining their conversation-based lives. I knew that however little or much people said or did, everything communicated. If somebody's mood was in question and I suspected I was missing cues, I made up possibilities or asked whomever was with me what they saw happening. I thought it would be easy for me to write down what I heard. I listen so carefully—talk so much—know letters and can ask about spelling when I have to. Surely the complexities of writing would come as naturally to me as had the intricacies of speaking.

My "insider language" included every feature and job that thinking, remembering, imagining, intuiting, or dreaming could do. It's everything within me that runs how I operate in life. Hmmm, I wondered, this might be harder. How will I figure all of them out; how will I get them into writing; how will I make good use of page space?

As a young student, I learned to print (unwieldy), write cursive (flowing shapes but slow to achieve), braille (noisy) and typewrite (mechanically efficient). In my late twenties and early thirties, as part of earning my Advanced Canadian Amateur Radio license, I learned Morse code.

In my mid forties, I learned to write with a computer. What a breakthrough. Here, at my fingertips, I have the most accessible combination of technology and software supporting me and whatever I write. Only while using a computer can I produce correctly spelled, grammatically organized, written concepts on a page. I can manipulate so much more of my own writing process and attempt the critical thinking that happens while revising. Then, magic moments, I can even dare trying different fonts, forms and styles, that is, if I know the keyboard commands that direct my screen reading program, JAWS, to tell me what I'm doing. But let's back up just a minute to when this all started.

Writing began with my feeling large print letters made from sandpaper glued onto card stock flash cards. "Janie, this shape is the letter A. It makes these sounds." Then, big, preschool muscles copied print letter shapes in air, accompanied by big mouth chants of "big A, little a," and on it went. I didn't like print letters—too sharp-edged, disproportionate, and disconnected. I pictured a page full of print as if it were a tray full of loose nuts and bolts. Today, my mental picture of print compares to the whitewater noise, off-balance experience I sometimes feel as a woman who is blind in a seeing world.

"What about cursive writing?" pondered the interested, concerned and committed adults in my life. "It'll probably work better. Let's give it a whirl." I feel my family's fingers drawing letters on my back and hands. Letters take shape in my mind and body. I chug my cursive name, Jane Livingston Turner, like a twenty car train on a circuitous route through the space in our house. I fling fluid shapes of cursive script about in space—they're reasonable and safe because they're connected. Next, small muscles grasp and control pens and pencils. Soon I arrived at paper with raised lines to serve as writing guides.

At first, graphite pencil points dragged in rough tugs along my paper. Pens skimmed or skittered out of control. As I improved, I loved signing my own library cards, art projects and other schoolwork. Later, I reveled in signing my own checks, college or employment applications. Though print and cursive writing work for getting signatures on their lines, they are too slow to be efficient writing processes for me.

Concurrent with print writing, braille writing and reading became part of my life during first, second and third grades. I reacted strongly and immediately. I didn't like those dumb little dots and those smelly ribbon-string bookmarkers in big books that draped my lap or hung over my desktop. Nobody else in my public school read or wrote like that! Not even Mary. I didn't like the braillewriter machine, either—too noisy! I pounded out plenty of aggression on Perkins Braillewriter keys during early braille lessons. Initially, I didn't have any fun picturing ideas compressed into smudgy, tight braille dot clumps. I wanted to rub those dots into oblivion! Once I began to learn cursive, I preferred picturing experiences in those fluid writing swirls. My attitude toward braille finally changed years later when I read this observation: "Braille is the only language that touches you back." Thanks, Jim Phigpen, for sharing this thought. It comforts me today; it offers healing for the past.

By fourth and fifth grade, print and cursive letters and braille word symbols were fairly clear in my mind; my hands could work within all three systems. Note: braille uses from one to six dot configurations, called cells, for its letter, part-word contractions, whole-word short forms, numbers and punctuation. These abbreviated words aid in meeting space requirements and shorten reading time.

Just for fun, I began picturing the shapes of print, cursive or braille symbols as matching forms of the objects or actions they represented. Making the best match became a great game for me. Imagine, this black fur and meat over bones, three-letter concept is dog. Printed letter dog parts stand alone in the world, like stick figures. Print creatures, can your letters cross those spaces to connect as friends? Cursive-writing dogs flow and fly. They swoop and soar with wings and tails—aren't cursive-writing dogs lovely? Finally, braille dogs are compact, efficient in all ways, like haiku poems—these groups of dots make the most of every inch. Give braille dogs an inch of space and these amazing, dot dog creatures give back miles of powerful meaning.

As a language reader, speaker, writer and an early childhood teaching assistant, when I learned braille in conjunction with English, my primary spoken language, it served as an efficient writing code. When I took French in high school, and later college Spanish, I discovered that most of the braille contractions and short forms to which I was accustomed didn't work. It never occurred to me that braille as I knew it couldn't easily transfer to French or Spanish. I had to newly learn how to use braille; two languages for the price of one.

I still read and write braille today. I believe that all language users must be as skilled in as many language tasks as they can. I believe it is important to be a literate listener, speaker, reader and writer. Though I work at a computer keyboard almost exclusively, my personal notes still clatter onto now beloved Perkins Braille-writer keys whenever I take messages on our home and office phones or make lists. I'm seeing to it that our sighted grand-children experiment with writing and touching braille—maybe reading print and braille later. Why not?

But in fourth grade, typewriting became my preferred writing method. As a typist, I felt better integrated into the world where seeing is the top dog. I discovered that, usually, there are fewer steps between typists and readers than exist between readers and braille writers. When I brailled schoolwork, I either had to read it aloud for my teachers and class, or my braille teacher had to print above my braille before others could understand.

During my pre-typing school days, sometimes-lazy Janie got away with covering her unpreparedness with braille-writing-noise that only I or my braille teacher could interpret. Further, I was free to remember braille word contractions and could conveniently forget letter components in words. The braille contraction for the word "with" is formed by pressing five of the six braille writer keys at once. This creates the everything-but-dot-one word symbol. As a print typist, I really had to learn to spell! My typist's life provided no hiding place for these habits; everybody saw whatever I typed. I certainly did not want to be exposed by a silent typewriter while others smugly used pencils or pens to scrawl "presidential" on our fourth grade spelling test. No more braille spelling shortcuts for me. To properly spell and type "with" in print, you have to know four letters and separately tap four keys: "w", "i", "t", "h", and this is just one of hundreds of examples.

For thirty-three years, writing worked like this: I typed, print readers read, made corrections, then read my writing out loud to me. This was my on-the-spot chance to braille, tape, or dictate revisions, and God forbid I should think more slowly than our scheduled hour of reading time allowed. Next, print readers taped the writing. I listened and rewrote again. The process was fragmented, frustrating, and tedious. It was rarely my own; it belonged to others too soon and too much of the time.

Owning a portable typewriter increased my sense of personal freedom to some degree; I could carry it with me and write wherever/whenever I wished. Still, writing felt like a pressure cooker. External stresses on my writing life included comments like, "Jane! You're bothering us with that disgusting typewriter noise. It's two o'clock in the blanking morning!" I desperately needed a way to type that wouldn't disturb others. I needed uninterrupted time to figure out what I really meant to say and write into being. Even if I taped or brailled initial thoughts, somewhere in the process I still had to work with readers. I hated it when my writing process didn't feel like my own; just too many people involved here too soon. What is appropriate reader help? How can I limit their time? Can I work more without them? For years, these were unanswered questions, and situations without solutions.

In 1990/91, I turned on my first computer, heard my first screen reader program's digitally correct voice, and burst into tears.

"I'll never understand this flat-toned, passionless babble!" I wailed.

"Technological miracles do happen," my instructor assured, "even for you, Jane."

I listened, comprehended, took an eager, anxious breath, rubbed my hands together, dug in and cranked up the reading speed. As I grew familiar with my computer, I found myself beginning to write—really write!

Nothing holds me back from writing anymore. No excuses now. I was ready to write, wasn't I? Wrong. Now, I must dig in and do it. If I want to write, I must keep my mind alert, and be willing to learn through experience, classes, and practice, practice, practice. Making computer equipment and software programs work for me is an ongoing task. My hands keep on learning new keyboard keys and keystroke pathways for getting my writing done. Note: totally blind computer users do not use a mouse, and visually oriented internet web sites are a real challenge.

Before I acquired computer skills, I felt overwhelmed and preoccupied by the mechanics of writing. Today, computers let me create new files and folders, move and work among them simultaneously, physically walk away, return and find everything right where I left it—where did I store that poem, anyway?—and make use of blank page space in a multitude of various letter colors and styles, fonts and formats. Gone for the most part are the days of bulky notebooks and big braille pages. Gone, to a significant extent, are the hassles involved in coordinating reader schedules to mine. And if I believed in more than the God in whom I trust, they'd be the gods of Spell and Grammar Check!

When I began writing, I had few notions of all that writing really involved and fewer notions of how much of it I could accomplish with computer technology at my fingertips. But today, technology places much more of my writing process in my hands. Revising (the art of rethinking and shaping) is new to me every day, and I love it. It is my proving ground. I focus my energies by rereading what is already written. Sometimes I get tired of how often I rewrite to clarify an idea. I ask myself, what did you think you said? What might you say? Now and then I just push back my chair with an "I don't know," "I don't care right now," or a "Maybe tomorrow."

Ultimately, the goal of revision, I think, is picking one best way of saying a thing. Editing (the art of paring down) was new to me, and it's a harder love to have. Since over-writing is my challenge, editing is an even bigger one. Editing out some "gem" makes me picture myself as Miss Scarlet murdering Colonel Mustard with the wrench in the Clue game's library. Revising and editing go hand in hand. They are the hard-worked shovels I use to muck out a good story so that characters and ideas, feelings and actions stand clear. Why are my favorite visualizations of editing tools hoes, rakes, shears, shovels and wheelbarrows? I glory in the work and pleasure of speaking through writing, any time of day. Keyboards type in luxurious silence. Here's to revising, where, on good days, I dig up nuggets of what could matter, and on many more I unapologetically gag then hope I can edit them all away.

I make lots of mistakes. But now, technology doesn't scare me so much anymore. With some equanimity, I face my mistakes. I fix some, and learn through some. I want to get the most from my computer programs and myself. I give thanks for human and tutorial technical supports that substantially increase my productivity.

Free writing is a new experience for me. I come to my desk alone. Let my hands trail in from the front outside corners of the desk to find, then dare to rest upon the keyboard. Alone, without others to help my writing, I am astounded and impressed because, though filled with trepidation at times, I feel brave. My fingers (like my mind) may poise in readiness. Mind and fingers may fidget. But, they don't leave. I know that I can sit as little or long as I wish before writing a blessed or blasted thing. Sometimes my hands are all fired up to lead me into the writing process. What'll it be today: some vague idea or theme to explore, dream or memory to imagine into my here and now, proposition or stipulation to develop, some demon to exercise or angel to reckon with, a question to ask or letter to write? I set the timer, sit down at the keys, shut my eyes, open my mind, and start typing. Wow! I get to finally be reckless! Yes! Today when I free write, I find out who I am, who I don't want to be, and, sometimes, how to get myself out of the way of the writing. When I free write and ideas do not come, I comfort myself with familiar rhythms as I copy song lyrics, favorite poems, and nursery rhymes. This kind of exercise is essential to my writing now.

When I cannot figure out what I want to say, not to mention the best way to say it, or which form or style to use, I invite comments and questions from others. I ask, "How have others expressed this idea or feeling?" I ask, "Can I create a woman's tears in words? Can fonts or formats be used to accentuate this, or will they distract readers?" Gone now, the embarrassment of my pre-computer times when sighted others had to help me with all steps of my writing. Today, choices about my writing are mine. I proudly welcome doing more of my work independently. When readers and I convene, I meet them with happy anticipation, readiness and pride to receive gifts that can best be given through human sharing. Initially I had to have readers partly because I wasn't confident of my writing until I heard it read in out loud. As I've grown more certain in my own speaking and thinking in writing, my relationship to readers is evolving. Now, when I hear readers reading what I have written, they give me gifts—the sound of my writing in a human, not computer generated, voice. The neatest thing of all is that they don't give me back the whole process of writing; now they can assist me with particular, smaller details; it's a more mutual give and take. They're not in charge of the basic writing—I am.

For years now, computers have assisted me. I hear and "see," experience and handle writing and reading more like my writing peers do. I "see" how writing fits and looks on the page. With a computer, I can write and read more efficiently. Today, I give thanks for the access to reading and writing that computers give. I celebrate the confidence and competence with which I am increasingly able to write. Today I know that writing is powerful, and it gives me a voice that can travel where I may never get to go.

CHAPTER SIX

Journey toward Wholeness: the Process

On one hand, many of my life experiences fit together like a basket's strands. Tightly woven, they shape me toward high function and fullest expression. No clutter there. Yet, given my culture's biases—"Able Bodies 'R Us"—uncertainty, anger and resignation thread distress through this basket of my life. Uncertainty: Is anything I do going to make it OK for me to be here—make me acceptable as a contributor? Anger: No matter how hard I work, my difference disturbs the culture's norms, and it's my fault. Resignation: I'm doing all that I can and I don't believe there is anything more I can do. Underneath my well styled, neatly dressed and cared for, formally educated and highly skilled exterior, these undercurrents have sometimes escalated into nasty undertows. They speak plainly through knots of tension in my muscles, furtive insider discussions within my mind and spirit, chewed nails and picked cuticles. These currents shaped themselves as—what else of course?—nagging questions. Am I merely a hodgepodge of unacceptable and abnormal, disconnected and devalued fragments that, somehow, one day, might magically click together? Will I ever be fully welcomed in society?

Wholeness is accepting myself as complete and enough—exactly right—normal for me—properly outfitted for life's journey—and blind. People have said to me, "Now that I know you, I don't even think of you as blind." I understand their effort to compliment me, to fit me to their world, but what those statements really do is significantly negate who I am and much of what's shaped my being. I want to tell them that they don't know me—all of me. I came the hard way to this cornerstone truth—I am whole for me, and wholeness includes my blindness.

Like preschoolers all across America, I first experienced my existence as the center of the universe. As a very young child, I loved hearing, understanding, speaking and singing life into being in song language. I thrilled to grow tall enough to reach doorknobs and kitchen counters, to help carry groceries in from the car and push laundry baskets to specified spots while naming each object and action. I had an extended busy family of nine to love and know. Exploring people, plants and animals, my home and neighborhood established in me a confidence, love of learning and determination to know things. Experiencing my early world as positive was a great good fortune—one that not all children get.

I understood myself to be an "asking why" child. I recognized myself as a meticulous cataloger, organizer and user of information. At others' homes, in stores or in doctors' offices, at meetings or when we heard something important on the car radio, Mom often said, "Janie, will you remember that for me?" I felt I had important information to keep track of and share, songs to sing, stories to tell. But for the slow-downs of my two pneumonia hospitalizations, the case of mumps which kept me from spending family time at the beach one summer, my three eye surgeries and the two weeks I spent at home recovering from a face-first slide down a gravel embankment, I was rarely sick and never immobile. As a youngster, I often listened only long enough to know who approached, to hear where things were located, to determine if the coast was clear, or to name a sound. Confident, glad, and purposeful summed up my feelings toward how I did the jobs I performed. I felt right in the world and that the world belonged to me. The only secrets in our house were events I hadn't witnessed or participated in, or glances that I perceived were happening but couldn't always interpret.

I don't remember whether or not we Turners ate apples every day, but I do know there were plenty around from our great old back yard tree. I handled apples, thought about them, learned from them, and applied some of what I learned to my life. Unlike apples, I had no stems. Like them, I had outside color, texture and temperature. I came with shape, size, weight and functions. I was full of good things; I knew about bad spots, too.

As a child who was nearly totally blind, for me learning needed to include an up-close and sometimes too personal sense of touch. I never remember a time in my life that was free of the question as to whether touch was or was not allowed as a way to learn. If others said touching was okay, it was. Why couldn't I, too, decide when or how I gathered information? When I initiated touch exploration to validate information presented verbally, I was often rebuked. Other motives, sexual curiosity for instance, were too often ascribed to my investigations. Throughout my life, sighted others often used their hands to touch me—without explaining why, or asking my permission. Why could they put me places or grab my hand to drag me along? I wanted to be touched as carefully, as respectfully, as reverently as books or money, as records or babies or flowers. I remember my childhood reaction to others' unwanted physical control—I expressed frustration and fury physically. I resisted; dug in my feet. I put on a sourpuss face and hung on the controlling hand as if I were a heavy suitcase. I wish they had asked what I would like.

As an adult, I often wish that, rather than assuming they know what I need, others would take time to learn and ask how, if at all, they might assist me today. What information, if any, do I need? I have learned that I need to lay it out plainly for you see-ers. Do not attempt to orient yourself to me by reaching out and grabbing me to position me to face you. A brief touch on my upper arm or forearm suffices. Do not grab my hands and direct them to see things without asking first. I'll pull my hands back. I'll push your hands away without apology. I will gather information in ways I deem appropriate at the time. I will decide which way to go about seeing. Touch is but one of my information gathering skills. I do not use this way of seeing casually; I am not careless with it. I, not you, get to decide when, where, how and which information gathering technique I will use at any given time. Rather than presuming I need to know what you see in order not to miss something, hush, wait, invite. When you see me looking for something with my hands, just let me look rather than saying "Let me get it" or "What are you looking for?" My looking may take longer. Can you give me the gift of time?

Let me illustrate how looking with my hands works:

1. With my hand or hands extended and a smile on my face, I say to young children, "Will you let my hands see what you're holding?" When, if they hesitate, I add, "After my hands explore it, I'll give it right back."

As soon as understanding and trust are established, I switch from see to touch. "May I touch it, explore it for a minute?" Often the whole dialogue shortens to "Hey, my turn, my turn," with hands eager, ready, open and waiting.

Children learn quickly—actions can be words after all. Can we adults sit up and take lessons? Yes, we can. Ask my grandchildren. They'll tell—no, they'll show you. Kaylie and Vincent, Felicia and Zandra already experientially know this. Words and actions lead to abstract yet concrete trust that accepts seeing in different ways. Where learning is invited, confidence and competence can be gained.

2. When my hands need to work with unfamiliar equipment, machines or areas of operation, I come to the borders of the area or thing and begin an unhurried, thorough investigation in all directions. Do not confuse meticulous exploration with groping. They are not the same.

3. Occasionally (and I do mean occasionally, since I have so many other ways of gathering information about people), I ask someone "May I have a look at you?" If their answer is "yes," I start by stepping close, standing still, and facing them, to better sense their energies. I keep my skimming touch neutral and specific, telling them what my hands seek to know. Do not think I'm out to hit on you. If I were to do that, I'd tell you, show you, and you'd know it. Further, do not think you can excuse your own inappropriate touch of me by saying, "I just wanted you to see…" whatever it was. Trust me, I'll know it and let you know about it sooner or later.

I love to see with my hands, picture my hands at work efficiently gathering information. They can be fearless and bold, social and political hands—hands reclaiming their right to see on their own terms. With purposeful, powerful strokes, jubilant hands work together and sweep away confusions caused by our culture's lingering preference for separate schools, housing and closed workshops where many blind individuals still exist. No more hands that grope, fumble or stumble as they see to gather information, perform tasks or explore. Their being and doing speak with respect, authority and skill. The choice to use my hands brings me personal worth, dignity, freedom and wholeness. My hands are not passive in a world that would like them to be. My hands have just as much right to see for me as your eyes do for you.

Sighted others still manage to make me worry that I, without sight, might miss something important along the way. I hated the knowledge that silent see-ers, without permission, could use their eyes to spy on me. Sometimes I felt their snooping probed me to the core.

In childhood, I tried reporting to adults how it felt. "He's staring at me… somebody's looking at me. Make them stop. It feels like poking." Now and again, an adult chided the silent snoop. "Don't tease by staring." More often than not, however, seeing was defended as, "It's OK. They're just looking".

From early childhood I understood that names mattered. I felt definite and plainly visible when people said or sang my name in songs. The descriptive names and nicknames my family had for me helped tell my story. I was called "Jane, Jane, The Worm," because one day a Pacific Ocean undertow dragged me down to the bottom of a tide pool, and I came up spitting sand and salt water with my hands filled with sea life, including the particular type of worm my researcher older sister, Anne, wanted to study. She also honored me by calling me "Sarah Jane" or "Jane Jane"—titles from old folk songs that celebrated the singing I loved to do. My mother occasionally called my twin sister "the ant" (she was such a steady worker) and me "the grasshopper", worried that I might never stop jumping from one thing to the other without finishing. I felt my leaps were curiosity at work.

When Daddy called me "Pumpkin Janie," or "Princess," his tone of voice was contradictorily full of disturbances that I couldn't begin to name back then. Was that shame, sorrow, guilt, embarrassment, fury I was hearing? I chose to hang onto the pet names, and leave the rest for another time.

When we girls were young, we were simply Mary and Jane to one another. In our adult years, my twin prefers to be identified by her full name, Mary Lee. She calls me Jane or, with deep affection now, "my Seester."

I learned some of my first math by considering Mary and me as individuals and twins. Counting out loud, I'd say, "1 whole Mary or 1 whole twin + 1 Jane (the other twin) = 2 whole girls, 2 whole twins who are parts of one whole pair—and that's a group."

When we started school, I was surprised when what we were became the names by which we were called. The kindergarten kids named me "blind girl" or "blind kid". The teacher called Mary and me "Twin," or "The twins!" "You Twins," Miss Grant, our kindergarten teacher hissed or bellowed, "Time for you to go with the eighth graders to walk the halls." This was her method of getting rid of us for a while. Insulted, embarrassed, infuriated, I wasn't sure which. However, the tendency to identify people without asking how they want to be labeled still gives me the creeps. I felt as if I were a piece of newspaper crumpled and thrown into our fireplace. Only sometimes did that teacher remember me as Jane.

In early childhood, Mary and I were close—a pair of strong individuals in a single unit. Between kindergarten and adulthood, we fought to achieve our own individual identities. We didn't want the lumped-together status inherent in how twins are often treated. We did not keep close because separateness appeared to be the most effective way to declare our individuality. Yet at what cost? We lost our connection. Now we've become close once more—plan on keeping close for the rest of our lives. Today, we challenge our culture not to dismiss or diminish twins with inappropriate labeling.

Throughout my early years, yet another two-faced tangle of likenesses and differences contributed to, or detracted from my sense of being personally outfitted for life's journey. It had to do with friends who were blind. Beyond my twin, we were not encouraged to have such friendships. Being at ease within my family, with lots of other friendly adults to validate me in my life, was not enough for me. I wished for at least some blind friends my own age with whom I could laugh or cry over learning braille, bumping into things, the hated feel of wearing glasses that didn't help me see, though they protected my eyes. I wanted to be able to talk to a friend about twin stuff in my life: separating us in school, dressing similarly or not as we chose, and the like.

When, in my mid thirties I chose to seek out and develop friendships with other disabled folks, it took me years to unashamedly share the realities of my blindness with these significant others; it took more time for me to let myself appreciate learning with and from them. Because of these kinship ties, I more completely accept and enjoy, celebrate and take responsibility for my whole self; I like this all-around happier person better!

Once I began developing such friendships, I was eager to learn what protocols made differences to folks with other disabilities. The day I planned on meeting Wendy, a former concert pianist who is deaf, now a University of Minnesota student, I was ready. I knew to keep myself (especially my face) always visible, and not get distracted by the nearby sign language interpreter.

"Hi, I'm Wendy," a deep male voice said.

Yipes! Nobody had prepared me for this turn of events. I'd assumed—how did that notion emerge?—that interpreters and clients would always be the same gender. Now I must delve into my own gender-biased language use. No more "how's it hanging?" without being certain with whom I spoke.

Once I had these friendships, I found that the benefits were many. They all came back to freedoms to be and to learn about others who walked marginal paths in society. I became eager to understand how my journey with an obvious physical disability paralleled or countered journeys of those who live with hidden disabilities or who experience discrimination because of some piece of their identity. For example, other than as an ally, I realized that I couldn't directly walk in the shoes of people whose color was different than mine. I could, however, gain experience about identity with an attempt to travel the path of a person with what I thought of as a less visible marker: that of being gay or lesbian. Sexual orientation differences do happen across all social groups. I asked friends what I needed to know about particular identifiers such as dress, body language, gestures and eye contact—lots of eye gazing—key spoken words and other things such as pop culture stuff: songs, plays, books and the like. I decided that the less pretence the better. I slipped off my wedding ring, "came out", and stayed out for 10 weeks as part of a project for the U of M's Diversity Institute.

Though I thought myself prepared to handle discrimination, I was shocked by blatantly expressed, irrational dislike and snubbing. A favorite bus driver decided he was too busy to talk with me any longer. Fellow students asked if I would get divorced. As a person who is disabled, the cultural bias I'd usually experienced around my physical blindness came down on the side of less cruel, more paternalistic—kindness tinged with the bad taste of way too much benevolence. Pity over what is percieved and handled as my loss was pervasive. Instances of hate directed to me as a blind woman were far rarer than what I experienced during this simulation as a lesbian woman.

Ever since that ten-week internship, I have given much consideration to similarities and differences between obvious or hidden disabilities and cultural challenges. I came to some new and clear understandings about costs people pay for passing or coming out. I learned that, if a person wants to, they can even hide behind educated sounding talk for self protection.

As a group facilitator and teacher, I have used simulations to promote the exploration of blindness. Caution and care are necessities; if simulations are used casually, without adequate introduction, they can and do reinforce negative stereotypes such as dependency, isolation and helplessness.

In such a simulation, I first provide individuals with sleep shades, formally called occluders, to wear. These mask-like creations completely block light. I invite groups to divide themselves into occluder wearers and non wearers. Group names such as Seers, Nonseers or No-See-'ems often quickly and spontaneously, sometimes a little desperately, emerge. How we humans struggle to belong.

I offer a few suggestions about whole body interaction with the environment: Make use of your hearing and voice to check sound differences. Utilize hands and arms for cross-body protection. Let your hands explore items you encounter or trail object edges. Let your feet follow carpet or flooring surfaces for orientation and directional cues. Don't forget your senses of touch, taste and smell; they can pick up plenty of useful information. Make room for your mind to engage in the work it's about to do—let the rest of your ways of knowing gather information.

Then come the rules—there are usually about three:

1. Nobody helps anybody else unless asked.

2. Do not touch anybody without permission. Now and then collisions happen. "Nice to bump into you today," I say.

3. Absolutely nobody gives assistance in any way unless clear about what the request is. If you can't provide what's asked for, it's okay to refuse. Brainstorm other possibilities. Offer to direct another assistant their way, or to give them directions to other information sources.

"Everybody ready? Okay! Let's do it," I say.

I assign them tasks: to go on break, find their ways to and from bathrooms, get their snacks and reconvene on time.

During these activities, folks may formulate some blindness-specific etiquette. They surmise things about what living blind might be. Most of all, people discover things about themselves as whole people when challenged to respond to life's changes and differences. Initially, individuals and groups often find that they're less gracious and more concerned with resisting change than they welcome it; they also struggle with how much time everything takes. Topics of conversation after such events often include: "How'd it work for you to have one of your familiar ways of operating changed or missing? What did you fear or find assurance in today? How did you manage gathering and using information while getting around? How did you feel when that unknown person touched you and wouldn't quit?" We talk about who partnered with whom and how much choice there was in partner selection. I ask about self trust: was yours lacking or on the rise?

Following twenty to forty-five minutes worth of simulation activity, space opens for genuinely amazing, though tough, conversations about how to live with what's in your lives. This kind of learning is truly valuable I believe.

Out of my life experiences as a person with disabilities, and a facilitator of and participant in awareness simulations, come the following questions that I would like to be asked more often: "What brings you here today? By what name would you like me to address you? What information, if any, would you like? How, if at all, may I assist you? How does this work for you?" I call these inclusion questions; they open up rather than shut down conversation.

Today, I have allowed blindness to take her good place in me. I like her in my life. Now and again I chuckle at the memory of my high school years when I wanted blindness to sit like a rock at the bottom of the otherwise good pond of my life. Too often, my living blind questions had camped out in "why me," rather than "why not me" locations. Now blindness has become a strong molder of my identity. She certainly shapes some of my creativity, sustains much of my personal discipline, directs my energy and growth. She focuses plenty of the work I choose to do. Blindness forces me to claim a larger sense of self. She has pushed open many kinds of doors.

I now believe that I look strong, happy and proud. With courage, I seek to understand my own fears, diminish ignorance by learning. I am more at ease with human differences; I relish, respect and include having these essential resources in my life. I understand that wholeness is a daily process and imperfection is as perfect a whole as any of us will ever become.

I love the images I have found for myself. An apple is a favorite image for my being; a sturdy, gnarled bonsai tree depicts my alternative body. Being as helpless as a Mack truck, as strong as a feather, are two more. When I speak out to advocate for myself and others, I imagine a bell ringing.

Not until I returned to school as a student at the University of Minnesota was I able to begin participating in conversations and expressing thoughts in speaking and writing about the process of wholeness in my life. My thoughts went to conflict and change, individuality, friendships and communities, my personal geographies and my cultural belonging. Reflective parts of my mind and spirit began shaping adages. Here's a sampling:

- Make friends with your body.
- My body is my home on earth.
- Delight in your body.
- I am, you are, "fearfully and wonderfully made."
- Imagine trustworthy pictures of yourself and your being.

- Welcome human similarities and differences.
- Understand that where differences are, conflict will be.
- When you can, welcome conflict as a positive experience. Be curious about it.
- Let conflict prompt consideration, questions and conversations.
- Accepting the things that cannot change and those that can is not always easy, but it is important.
- Let language create and sustain life in you and for you.
- Alone in the world? No! You belong to communities.
- Help others and let them help you.

This last adage has been most challenging for me. It has helped to remember what South American educator Paulo Freire declared: "Authentic help means that all who are involved help each other mutually, growing together in the common effort to understand the reality which they seek to transform. Only (then) can the act of helping become free from the distortion in which the helper dominates the helped."

How often have people assumed that I couldn't offer or be trusted to give help, but that they without question had to help me? So I say, make friends with different others; help people and let them help you. Helping one another gives us all life-giving gifts of equality in meeting needs and having our needs met. I do not have to do it alone. That particular brand of rugged independence at any cost doesn't work! What does work is what I call creative interdependence.

In my poem "After We Meet," I stated that my disability was an accident. Yet, for me, living blind is no accident. It is part of my whole self. I have had to remember often what my friend, Gene Chelberg, said with such conviction: "When our culture considers disability an expected part of human experience, then people with disabilities will identify proudly and with dignity beyond disability as crisis."

I'm proud and glad to be in this world today just as I am—because of and inclusive of my disability. Within my culture now, there are many disability aids for the blind. These include and are not limited to library books in braille or on tape or accessible via computer scanners. Theatre productions, movies and other media programs can be accompanied with descriptive services. Much more public transportation is available than when I was young. Bus drivers are mandated to call out stops. When I go to vote, I can accomplish it independently with the assistance of election judges. Public buildings display alternatively formatted signage. These all are important accomplishments. Then, there is policy and law; all of the civil, human rights legislation—topped by the Americans with Disabilities Act and subsequent clarifying legislation. It is up to us all to keep on working together toward creating accessible social, physical, political, educational, employment and economic space for all members of society. Today the very experience of blindness that disconnected me from myself and my society gives me reason for being and connections that make me whole.

That Bonsai tree image for this self-in-process person I am teaches me that I have many strong life-giving roots. Perhaps by now, like me, you will not be surprised to find that strengthening, in large measures, comes from where you have struggled. It has been hard for me to accept help. Blessings come when I do. It is tough to accept the permanence of my disability. Wholeness and joy and self worth come when I can. Maybe now, like me, you, too, can recognize that those cultural markers of age, class, color, disability, etc., apply to you. They are your self-in-process tree roots. They connect you with life experience and communities. How you handle them nourishes your branches.

CHAPTER SEVEN

My Journey isn't Over Yet: What I Thought were Destinations are truly Stepping Stones

Here's to beginnings and endings, premature, on time, overdue, clear or indirect; to human beings who've shaped my life toward goodness and strength and self worth. You know who you are. Here's to the particular human likenesses and differences that have been life-shaping for me; to conflict which stirs my life pot; to change which merely uses past life events as basis for reinventing life's wheels. Here's to language that creates and sustains life; to language that brings new life by placing future possibilities into my present; to life's transformations, which come when we let language do her distinct work.

Here's to: walking with every white cane, dog guide, and sighted guide who've been part and parcel of my mobility. Here's to negotiating the physical world. To all the kinds of natural and urban environments I have experienced: fields and woods, lake shores, beaches, salt water, hot desert days and sharp cool nights, mountain trails and meadows. To myriad architectural challenges I have met: bridges, towers, hundreds of steps up to our Lady Liberty's Lamp, hundreds more to reach Ireland's Blarney Stone; to stadium bleachers, elevators and escalators; to all sorts of streets and, yes, median strips, construction sites, airports, bus and train stations; to the eleven schools I have attended, the three where I've worked, and all the schools I've visited as a speaker;

and to every kind of private and public bathroom. To every place I couldn't go, to every museum, movie or other presentation whose inaccessibility I challenged and achieved access. To every new piece of adaptive equipment and every new construction made accessible to more of us from the get-go.

Here's to the flow of days, nights and seasons of natural dark and light. To the sometimes frightening, sometimes delicious, not always safe yet often awesome experience of living blind and its outcome, BlindSight. To some poignant personal truths and the caring interest of others that I suspect I'd have ignored had disability not been here. To the evolutionary creation of DarkLight, my personal blend of natural light and dark. To the conversations and experiences through which these important inner clearings have been created and shared.

Here's to amazing Grace and all her angels; faith walking; infinite God and finite human—what alchemy, what mergers.

Here's to the distinctly unique, life-giving human experience of communicating with language through body silences, stillnesses, sounds or actions and facial expressions, through voice sounds and words and now, writing. Living blind has certainly challenged me to use them all. Now here's to every brave one of you individuals who's courageously stepped forward to ask me a burning question or make a bold statement; to all those who've authentically answered mine. May all of you find precise language to tell your stories in many ways and then give up whatever life stories get in the ways of your moving forward. May you make paths for peace—proactive peace that makes room for challenges rather than passively giving in or up. Life works best when we use language to place brand new possibilities into the here and now. Here's to transformations that come during life-giving conversations.

To all you travelers, wherever you are, whatever you face, you and I are just where we need to be right now. I challenge you to keep on keeping on. May all your journeys be authentic. May you experience arrivals that become thresholds or stepping stones, not end points. May you come to acknowledge and celebrate the mercies of your particular journey. You've joined me for these written dialogues; perhaps we will meet and talk together someday. I hope that you have discovered, as I have, that loads travel lighter because of conversations.

RECOMMENDED SERVICES, BOOK, FILM AND WEB RESOURCES

Services

Abbey Road Book Search
6930 West 25th Lakewood, CO 80214
303-462-2665

The Aurora Center for Advocacy and Education at the University of Minnesota
Provides free and confidential supportive services to victims and survivors of sexual assault, relationship violence, and stalking
410 Church St SE Ste 407
Boynton Health Services
Minneapolis, MN 55455
General number: (612) 626-2929
24 hour Crisis Line: (612) 626-9111
Web site: www.umn.edu/aurora

American Counsel of the Blind—ACB
Advocacy, policy and legislation
1155 15TH St. NW 1004 Washington DC 20005
Toll free: (800) 424-8666
Web site: www.acb.org

American Foundation for the Blind—AFB
Expanding possibilities for people with vision loss
11 Pennsylvania Plaza NYC, NY 10001
Toll free: (800) 232-5463
Web site: www.afb.org

American Kennel Club—AKC
Dedicated to upholding the integrity of its registry, promoting the sport of purebred dogs and breeding for type and function
5580 Centerview Drive Raleigh, NC 27606
212-696-8200 or 919-233-9767
Web site: www.akc.org

American Printing House for the Blind—APH
We are the center of knowledge regarding the research, development and production of quality products and the provision of specialized services for the blind and visually impaired.
1839 Frankfort AVE Louisville, KT 40206
Toll free: (800) 223-1839
Web site: www.aph.org

Descriptive Video Service—DVS
Media Access Group at WGBH
545 Fifth Avenue, Suite 609 New York, NY 10017
Toll free: (800) 333-1203
Web site: http://dvs.wgbh.org

Federation of the Blind—NFB
We fight for the equality of the blind.
1800 Johnson St. Baltimore, MD 21230
(410) 659-9314
Web site: www.nfb.org

Freedom Scientific Inc.
We gain your independence through creating technologies for reading, speaking writing, information processing and learning.
11800 34th CT N. Saint Petersburg, FL 33716-1805
Toll free: (800) 444-4443
Web site: www.freedomscientific.com

Guide Dog Users Incorporated—GDUI
An affiliate of the American Council of the Blind, the largest guide dog consumer driven group in the world
14311 Astrodome Drive Silver Spring, MD 20906
Toll-Free: 888-858-1008
Web site: http://www.gdui.org

Hadley School for the Blind
Hadley's mission is to promote independent living through lifelong, distance education programs for blind people, their families and blindness service providers.
700 Elm St. Winnetka, IL 60093
Toll free: (800) 526-9909
Web site: www.hadley.edu

Multiple Connections—formerly known as Twin Topics
Our club's mission is to help mothers of multiples find support, share parenting tips, participate in family outings, hear education speakers and most of all have a good time being a Mom.
Club phone: (952) 953-7365
Web site: www.multipleconnectionsmn.org

National Library Service for the Blind and Physically Handicapped
The Library of Congress
Provides braille and recorded books and magazines on free loan to eligible residents of the United States or American citizens living abroad who are unable to read standard print because of permanent or temporary visual or physical disabilities
1291 Taylor St NW Washington DC 20011
Toll free: 800-424-8567
Web site: www.loc.gov/nls/

National Braille Press—NBP
A nonprofit printer and publisher offering braille books, magazines, textbooks, tests and customized embossing services
88 ST. Stephen St. Boston, MA 02115
Toll free: (800) 548-7323 Local: (617) 266-6160
Web site: www.nbp.org

The Minnesota Library for the Blind and Physically Handicapped
Administers a free national library program for visually and physically disabled persons who cannot use normal print library materials
388 SE 6TH Ave. Faribault, MN 55021-6340
Toll free: 800-722-0550
Catalog web site: www.klas.com/mnbph
Regional library information web site:
www.education.state.mn.us/mde/learning_support/mn_library_ft_blind_handicapped/index.html

Living Justice Press —LJP, Denise Bretton, Executive Director
To publish and promote alternative works about social justice and community healing
2093 Juliet Avenue St. Paul, MN 55105
(651) 695-1008
Web site: www.livingjusticepress.org

Minnesota State Services for the Blind—SSB
To facilitate the achievement of vocational and personal independence by Minnesotans who are blind, visually impaired or DeafBlind
2200 University Ave. W. Suite 240 ST Paul, MN 55114-1840
651-642-0500
Communication Center: Minnesota Radio Talking Book Network
Web site: www.mnssb.org/allages/commcenter/rtb
Communication Center Audio Services
Web site: www.mnssb.org/allages/commcenter/tape.html
Communication Center Braille Section
Web site: www.mnssb.org/allages/commcenter/braille.html

Mobility International USA—MIUSA
The national clearinghouse on disability and exchange—NCDE
We help people with disabilities participate in international exchange programs and we assist exchange programs to accommodate people with disabilities
132 E. Broadway Eugene, OR 97401
(541) 343-1284
Web site: www.miusa.org

National Institute of Health
retinopathy of prematurity information
Web site: http://www.nei.nih.gov/health/rop/index.asp

North American Hunting Retriever Association—NAHRA
Conducts retriever events that foster and recognize excellence in the retriever as a hunter's companion and conservation animal
P.O. Box 5159 Fredericksburg, VA 22403
540-899-7620
Web site: www.nahranews.org

Northern Flight Hunting Retrievers Association—NFHRA
NFHRA promotes and educates the use and training of hunting retrievers as a conservation tool for sound management and use of all our upland game and water fowl
Deb Powell, Secretary
7275 2061st Ave NE Stacy, MN 55079
651-335-2840
Web site: www.northernflighthuntingretrieversassociation.com

Kay Pranis
Peacemaking, Keeping Restorative Justice seminars and writing
Promoting the use of restorative justice principles in the criminal justice system and communities by providing training and technical assistance to courts, corrections, schools, community groups.
www.restorativejustice.org

Schuler Shoes
1 Family. 4 Generations. Since 1889. Personal Fit Style
7835 Main St N. Ste 200 Maple Grove, MN 55369
(763) 494-0011
Web site: www.schulershoes.com

The Seeing Eye—TSE
To enhance the independence, dignity and self confidence of blind people through the use of Seeing Eye dogs
300 Washington Ave. Morristown, NJ 07963-0375
Toll free: (800) 539-4425
Web site: www.seeingeye.org

StirFry Seminars and Consulting—Lee Mun Wah President
We bridge attitudes and values to reflect and honor differences through dialogue.
2311 8TH St Berkeley, CA 94710
510-419-3930
Web site: http://www.stirfryseminars.com/

Building A Vocal Community—Ysaye M. Barnwell (a five day workshop)
Teaching the world to sing one community at a time
2441 Tunlaw Road NW Washington DC 20007
202-625-7870
Web site: www.ymbarnwell.com

Sweet Honey In The Rock
P.O. Box 32164 Washington DC 20007
202-399-6604
Web site: www.sweethoney.com

Yako Tahnahga, Indigenous Native American
We offer programs for healing Our Relationships With The Earth, The Spirit, The Plants, The Animals And Ourselves.
Mailing address for inquiries:
255 River Woods LN Burnsville, MN 55337

Triumph Technology LLC
We provide adaptive technology solutions for people who are blind or have low vision.
1349 Pike Lake Drive New Brighton, MN 55112
(651) 636-5184
Web site: www.triumphonic.com

Women's Legacies Circles—Rachael Freed Educator, Facilitater and Author
To begin the process of creating your unique legacy for family, loved ones, and community
P.O. Box 16202 Minneapolis MN 55416
612-558-3331
Web site: www.womenslegacies.com

Valley Community Presbyterian Church
Open hearts—Open minds—Opening lives to God
3100 Lilac Drive Golden Valley, MN 55422
763-588-0831
Web site: www.valleychurch.net

Vision Loss Resources—VLR
A multifaceted organization which provides comprehensive training, equipment, and support services for blind and deaf-blind people of all ages
1936 Lyndale Ave S. Minneapolis, MN 55403
612-871-2222

Books

Breton, Denise
"Mystic Heart Of Justice: restoring wholeness in a broken world"
2001 by Swedenborg Foundation
ISBN: 0877853002 Pages: 321

Brown, Steven E. Ph.D.
"Movie Stars And Sensuous Scars: essays on the journey from disability shame to disability pride"
2003 by Universe
ISBN: 0595288936 Pages: 216

Champlin, Charles
"My friend, you are legally blind: a writer's struggle with macular degeneration"
2001 by John Daniel & Company Books
ISBN: 1880284480 Pages: 72

Dossett, Ellen
"Just As I Am: Americans With Disabilities"
1999 by Crane Hill
ISBN: 1575871149 Pages: 143

Fadiman, Anne
"The Spirit Catches You And You Fall Down: a Hmong child, her American doctors, and the collision of two cultures"
1997 by Farrar, Straus and Giroux
ISBN: 0374267812 Pages: 339

Finger, Anne
"Past Due: a story of disability, pregnancy, and birth"
1990 by Seal Press
ISBN: 0931188873 Pages: 203

Finger, Anne
"Basic Skills"
1988 by University of Missouri Press
ISBN: 082606573 Pages: 117 paperback

Finger, Anne
"Bone Truth"
1994 by Coffee House Press
ISBN: 1566890284 Pages: 192 paperback

Finke, Beth
"Long Time No See"
2003 by University of Illinois Press
ISBN: 0252028279 Pages: 204

Ford, Sallie Rochester
"Mary Bunyan: The Dreamer's Blind Daughter,"
1996 published by Grace & Truth Books (reprinted from1860 by Boston, Gould & Lincoln)
ISBN: 1583391320 Pages: 488

Freed, Rachael
"Women's Lives, Women's Legacies: passing your beliefs and blessings to future generations"
2003 by Fairview Press
ISBN: 157749119X Pages: 288

Freed, Rachael
"The Women's Legacies Workbook for the Busy Woman
2005 by Minerva Press
ISBN: 0-9637795-4-0 Pages: 136

Fries, Kenny
"Body, Remember: a memoir"
2003 by the University of Wisconsin Press
ISBN: 0299190544 Pages: 248

Fries, Kenny, Editor
"Staring Back: the disability experience from the inside out"
1997 by Plume Books
ISBN: 0452279135 Pages: 414

Gallagher, Hugh Gregory
"FDR's Splendid Deception: the moving story of Roosevelt's massive disability and the intense efforts to conceal it from the public"
1985 by Dodd Mead
ISBN: 0396085210 Pages: 250

Griffin, John Howard
"Scattered Shadows: a memoir of blindness and vision"
2004 by Orbis Books
ISBN: 1570755396 Pages: 230

Hockenberry, John
"Moving Violations: war zones, wheelchairs and declarations of independence"
1995 by Hyperion
ISBN: 0786860782 Pages: 371

Hull, John M.
"Touching The Rock: an experience of blindness"
1991 by Trinity Press International
ISBN: 0679401687 Pages: 218

Hull, John M.
"In The Beginning There Was Darkness: a blind person's conversations with the Bible"
2002 by Trinity Press International
ISBN: 1563383683 Pages: 176

Jamison, Kay Redfield
"An Unquiet Mind"
1995 by: A. A. Knopf
ISBN: 0679443746 Pages: 223

Kleege, Georgina
"Sight Unseen"
1999 by Yale University Press
ISBN: 0300076800 Pages: 233

Lamott, Anne
"Operating Instructions: a journal of my son's first year"
1993 by Pantheon
ISBN: 0679420916 Pages: 251

Linton, Simi
"Claiming Disability: knowledge and identity"
1998 by New York University Press
ISBN: 0814751334 Pages: 203

Linton, Simi
"My Body Politic: a memoir"
2005 by University of Michigan Press
ISBN: 0472115391 Pages: 256

Longmore, Paul K
"The New Disability History: American perspectives"
2001 by New York University Press
ISBN: 0814785638 Pages: 416

Longmore, Paul K
"Why I burned My Book And Other Essays On Disability"
2003 by Temple University Press
ISBN: 1592130232 Pages: 278

Lusseyran, Jacques
"And There Was Light: the autobiography of a blind hero of the French Resistance"
1998 by Morning Light
ISBN: 0930407407 Pages: 316

Mandel, Sally
"Out Of The Blue"
2000 by Ballantine Books
ISBN: 0345428900 Pages: 295

Michalko, Rod
"The Mystery of the Eye and the Shadow of Blindness"
1998 by University of Toronto Press
ISBN: 0802042503 Pages: 178

Michalko Rod
"The Difference That Disability Makes"
2002 by Temple University Press
ISBN: 1-56639 934-3 Pages: 194

Mehta, Ved
"Stolen Light: Continents of Exile" Vol. 6.
1987/8/9 by W W Norton & Co Inc
ISBN: 0393026329 Pages: 462

Morris, Jenny
"Pride Against Prejudice: transforming attitudes to disabilities"
1998 by the Women's Press
ISBN: 0704342863 Pages: 199

Norris, Kathleen
"Dakota: A spiritual geography"
1993 by Ticknor & Fields
ISBN: 0395633206 Pages: 224

Palmer, Parker J
"The Active Life: a spirituality of work, creativity and caring"
1990 by Jossey-Bass
ISBN: 0060664576 pages: 160

O'Brien, Mark
"How I Became A Human Being: a disabled man's quest for independence"
2003 by University of Wisconsin Press
ISBN: 0-299-18430-7 Pages: 263

Omvig, James H
"Freedom For The Blind: The Secret Is Empowerment"
2002 by Rehabilitation Continuing Education Program
University of Arkansas, Fayetteville,
Arkansas (The Critical Concerns in Blindness Series; 2.)
Pages: 158

Potok, Andrew
"Ordinary Daylight: Portrait Of An Artist Going Blind"
1980 by Holt, Rinehart, and Winston
ISBN: 0030298210 Pages: 290

Potok, Andrew
"A Matter Of Dignity: Changing the lives Of The Disabled"
2002 by Bantam Books
ISBN: 0553802151 Pages: 305

Pranis, Kay
"Peacemaking Circles: from crime to community"
2003 by Living Justice Press
ISBN: 0972188606. Pages: 250

Pranis, Kay
"Little Book Of Circle Processes: a new/old approach to peacemaking"
2005 by Good Books
ISBN: 1-56148-461-X Pages: 76

Remen, Rachel Naomi
"Kitchen Table Wisdom: stories that heal"
1996 by Riverhead Books
ISBN: 1573220426 Pages: 336

Roberts, Jason
"A Sense Of The World: how a blind man became history's greatest traveler"
2006 by HarperCollins
ISBN: 000716169 Pages: 400

Sanford, Matthew
"Waking: a memoir of trauma and transcendence"
2006 by Rodale Press
ISBN: 1594863024 Pages: 241

Schneider , Katherine
"To The Left Of Inspiration: adventures in living with disabilities"
2006 by Dog Ear Publishing
ISBN: 1598581317 Pages: 128

Shapiro, Joel
"No Pity: people with disabilities forging a new civil rights movement"
1994 by Crown Publishing Company
ISBN: 0812924126 Pages: 382

Simon, Rachel
"Riding The Bus With My Sister: a true life journey"
2003 by Plume
ISBN: 0452284554 Pages: 304

Skloot, Floyd
"In The Shadow of Memory"
2003 by University of Nebraska Press
ISBN: 0803242972 Pages: 243

Smith, Greg
"On A Roll"
1995 by On a Roll Communications
ISBN: 0976711109 Pages: 280

Solomon, Andrew
"The Noonday Demon: an atlas of depression"
2001, 2002 by Simon & Schuster
ISBN: 068485466-X Pages: 576

Soloman, Annie
"Blind Curve"
2005 by Wylin Soloman
ISBN: 0751536784 Pages: 366

Takaki, Ronald
"A Different Mirror: A history of multicultural America"
1993 by Little, Brown and Company
ISBN: 0316831123 Pages: 508

Vaughan, C. Edwin
"The Struggle Of Blind People For Self Determination, Social And Cultural Perspectives: Barriers To Community Integration"
1993 by C.C. Thomas
ISBN: 0398058547 Pages: 244

Wah, Lee Mun
"The Art of Mindful Facilitation"
2004 by Krishna Copy
Pages: 159

Wiggs, Susan
"Home Before Dark" 2003 by MIRA Books
ISBN: 1551666731 Pages: 378

York, Stacey
"Roots And Wings: Affirming culture in early childhood programs"
1991 by Redleaf Press
ISBN: 1929610327 Pages: 272

York, Stacey
"Big As Life: Vol 1. The everyday inclusive curriculum"
2004 by Redleaf Press
ISBN: 1884834396 Pages: 300
Vol. 2 ISBN: 1884834515 pages: 300

Zinn, Howard
"A People's History of the United States: 1492-present"
2003 by HarperCollins
ISBN: 0060528427 Pages: 729

Films

"Benny and Joon" 1993
Director: Jeremiah Chechik

"Color of Fear"—a documentary
StirFry Seminars and Consulting

"Coming Home" 1978
Directed by Hal Ashby

"Freedom Machines" 2005—documentary
PBS

"Gaby: a true story" 1997
Directed by Luis Mandoki

"Passion Fish" 1992.
Written and directed by: John Sayles

"Scent of a Woman" 1992
Director: Martin Brest

"Touch the Sound" 2004—documentary
Director: Thomas Riedelsheimer

"When Billy Broke His Head And Other Tales Of Wonder" 1995
Written and Edited by: Billy Galfus

Poems

All poems in this essay are the original work of Jane L. Toleno

Citations

Pg. 67: Marilyn Frye, "Oppression", The Politics of Reality (Trumansburg, N.Y.,: The Crossing Press, 1983)

Pg. 114: Gene Chelberg, Director
Disability Programs and Resource Center
San Francisco, State University
San Francisco, CA 94132

Song Lyrics

"Bigger than Any Mountain"; Gospel Echoes Prison Ministry Recording
composer: Gordon Jenson
P.O. Box 555 Goshen IN 46527
www.gospelechoes.com

Ms. Toleno also is published in:

Several articles in this magazine, including her poem "My Red Mittens":
DIALOGUE: A World of Ideas for Visually Impaired People of all Ages
Blindskills Inc.
700 Church street SE, Salem Oregon 97301

Article: "Fun, Fit, & Fifty Plus—My Saga of Inspiration and Motivation"
PALAESTRA, p. 29, Vol. 16, No. 4 (Fall, 2000)
http://www.palaestra.com

Article: "This Ground I Love"
Photographs by Brian Peterson
"Voices For The Land: Minnesotans write about the places they love" 2002 by MN Historical Society Press
ISBN: 0873514319 Pages: 116

Article: "Baskets"
Midwest Home & Garden magazine P162 08/02
Minnesota Monthly Magazine
Editing: Courtney Lewis (612) 371-5818

Article: "Baxter Retires"
Anderson, Allen and Linda
"Angel Animals: Exploring Our Spiritual Connection with Animals" 1999 by Plume
ISBN: 0452280729 Pages: 278